THE FRIEDMAN COLLECTION

ARTISTS OF CHICAGO

Published in the United States of America in 2002 by
Spanierman Gallery, LLC, 45 East 58th Street, New York, NY 10022.

Library of Congress Control Number: 2002101040

ISBN 0-945936-49-4

Design: Marcus Ratliff
Photography: Roz Akin
Composition: Amy Pyle
Color imaging: Center Page
Lithography: Meridian Printing

THE FRIEDMAN COLLECTION

—◆—

ARTISTS OF CHICAGO

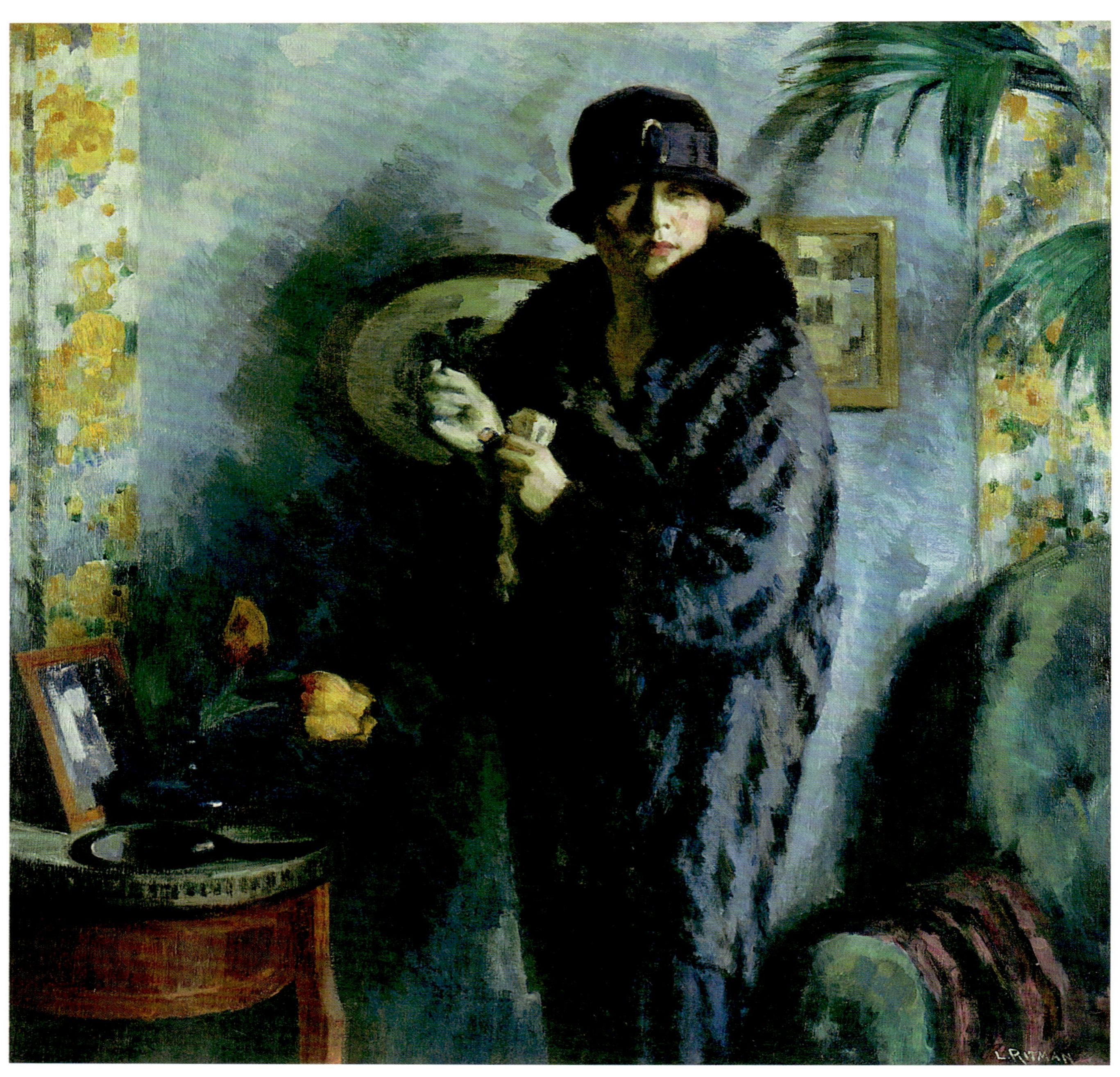

Louis Ritman (1889–1963)
Woman in a Fur Coat, ca. 1910s, oil on canvas, 38 × 39 inches

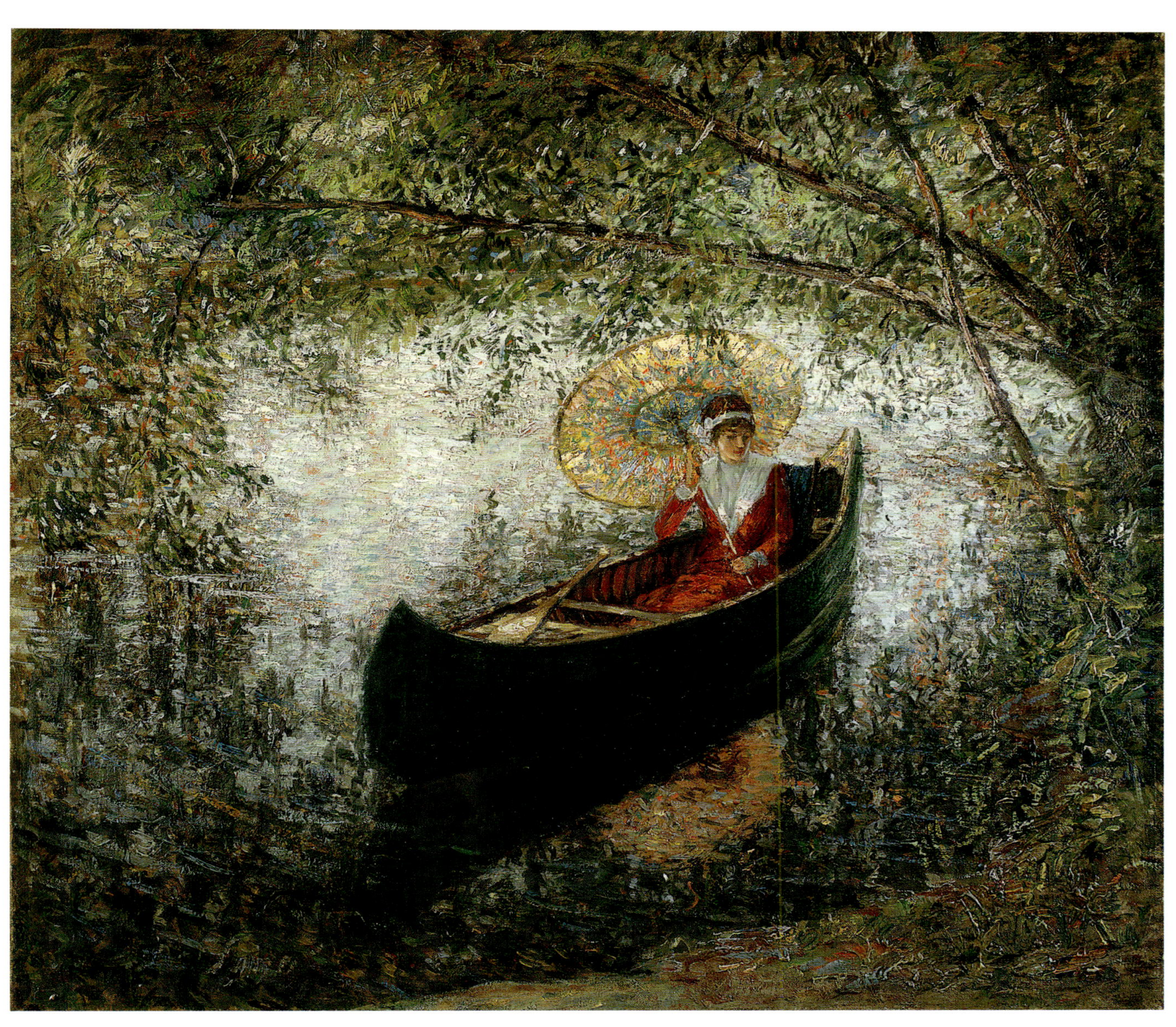

Wilson Henry Irvine (1869–1936)
In the Canoe, ca. 1900–20, oil on canvas, 24 × 27 inches

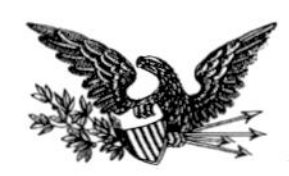

Spanierman Gallery, LLC

www.spanierman.com

45 East 58th Street   New York, NY 10022

Tel (212) 832-0208   Fax (212) 832-8114   gavin@spanierman.com

THE FRIEDMAN COLLECTION: ARTISTS OF CHICAGO

March 7 – April 6, 2002

Essay by Dr. William H. Gerdts

Spanierman Gallery, LLC

www.spanierman.com

45 East 58th Street   New York, NY 10022

Tel (212) 832-0208   Fax (212) 832-8114   gavin@spanierman.com

ACKNOWLEDGMENTS

One of the most enjoyable aspects of working in the gallery is the daily opportunity to learn. The James Friedman Collection has presented just such a chance. The works of art here include a broad and diverse cross-section of paintings by artists who were associated with the vibrant city of Chicago around the turn of the twentieth century, many of whom have been previously overlooked.

I was astonished when I became acquainted with the collection. Jim Friedman gathered it over the course of twenty years. With infectious passion, he sought to represent many facets of Chicago art, including works by artists who painted in and around the city and those who spent shorter periods of time in Chicago, having made their careers elsewhere. In addition, reflecting the mobility of artists at the beginning of the last century, there are works by artists who were based in Chicago, but who also frequently traveled far afield. The collection consists of landscapes, figural works, and city views and reflects many stylistic influences including the French Barbizon artists, Impressionists, Post-Impressionists, and Fauvists as well as the Ashcan School painters who were based in New York. It is with just such a wide-ranging survey that the richness of the art of a particular region can begin to be understood. We are glad to participate in the developing interest of the art created in different regions of our great country.

There are not enough ways to thank all of the people who have helped bring this project together. First and foremost I would like to express appreciation to Jim Friedman, whose dedication to the art of Chicago has provided this eye-opening opportunity. As always, Dr. William H. Gerdts has been an invaluable friend, and his insightful essay has pulled together the many strands of a complex regional flowering. Joel Dreyer, director of the Illinois Historical Art Project, also furnished important consultation, and his scholarship, which will culminate in a landmark publication on Illinois painters born before 1900, has established a basis for all further studies of Chicago art. Dr. Robert G. Bardin, Carol Lowrey, and Dr. Lisa N. Peters wrote the artists' biographies in this catalogue, many of which necessitated extensive research. Fronia Simpson was a conscientious editor, while Dr. Peters and Deborah Gerstler Spanierman oversaw the editorial process. I wish to thank Marcus Ratliff and Amy Pyle for their wonderful design. All other members of the Spanierman Gallery staff provided essential contributions to this effort. A special recognition is due to Rosalind Akin, William Fiddler, Matthew Fisher, Garth Freeman, and Christina Vassallo. Of course, I wish to express my gratitude to my father Ira Spanierman for his guidance.

Gavin Spanierman

The Friedman Collection:
Artists of Chicago

The interest in, and collecting of, American regional art of the past is a relatively recent phenomenon. Until a few decades ago the vast majority of collectors of historical American painting and sculpture concentrated on the art that was produced in the major northeastern metropolises. There were exceptions to this of course—Winslow Homer's great seascapes painted in Prout's Neck, Maine, at the turn of the twentieth century, or William Sidney Mount's genre scenes of rural Long Island rendered in the mid-nineteenth century. Most of the works that attracted collectors, both private and public, were produced in urban studios in Boston, Philadelphia, and especially New York, even if they depicted exotic landscapes of South America, such as those by Frederic Church, or presented dramatic vistas of the Rockies or Yosemite, such as those by Albert Bierstadt.

More recently, however, some collectors have begun to focus on the art produced in their home territories and in the process have brought to light painters, sculptors, and printmakers of considerable quality who had been nearly or even totally forgotten once their own often-flourishing careers came to an end. The art of some regions in this country have been more quickly investigated and collected than others. For several decades, there have developed literally hundreds, and perhaps thousands, of collectors of California art, scores of dealers who specialize in California painting, and several institutions devoted solely to its acquisition and exhibition. More recently, the art of the American South, previously totally ignored, has become of the focus of both collecting and scholarship, with increasing recognition given to the distinctions that lie within certain areas, for example, the art of Charleston or of New Orleans.

The near-Midwest has also witnessed a good deal of interest among collectors, dealers, scholars, and museums, but curiously, this has centered for the most part in Indiana and Ohio, where the local artistic heritage has been celebrated for quite some time. Commercial galleries in Indianapolis, Cincinnati, Columbus, and Cleveland have catered to those concerns, which have been both supported by, and supportive of, the local art institutions in those cities. In Illinois, interest in the art of the region, and in that of Chicago artists, is just now beginning to build. The Illinois Historical Art Project, instituted by the local collector, scholar, and art patron, Joel Dryer, promises a momentous study and dictionary of artists of the state and will fill a long-needed lacuna. Its publication is scheduled for 2010.[1] The important collection of Powell Bridges, *Chicago Paintings: 1895–1945*, went on exhibition at the Illinois State Museum in Springfield early in 2000.[2] Many of the Chicago artists whose works have appeared in that show are also included here in *The Friedman Collection of Chicago Artists* where, for the first time, a survey of Chicago painting may be seen in New York.

The Friedman Collection consists of work by Chicago painters from the late nineteenth through the mid-twentieth century, and is limited in its later decades to representational work rather than to that of the modernists who began to offer an alternative aesthetic vision on the cultural map of that city; ironically, exhibitions and scholarship that have taken place in the last several decades have been almost exclusively devoted to that modernist current and its development.[3] The principal exceptions within the Friedman Collection are several impressive paintings by American artists active in the artists' colony in Giverny, France, who worked there side by side with some of the Chicago painters of the early twentieth century. Overall the works amassed in the collection constitute an important and unusual regional achievement.

Chicago's artistic heritage, relative to that of major Eastern centers, is relatively brief; a few portrait and landscape painters were active there in the 1830s and 1840s, but it was only with the arrival in the city in 1855 of George Peter Alexander Healy, a portraitist of international reputation, that a strong professional artistic core began to develop. By the 1860s there was a lively artists' colony of portrait and landscape painters resident in Chicago, with an active Academy of Design serving both as a school and an exhibition venue, but all that was lost in the great fire of October, 1871. Some of the leading local painters left the city permanently; others had already departed for study abroad in Paris or in Munich, the latter especially popular with painters from cities in the Midwest with large German populations.

One of the most notable was Walter Shirlaw, represented here with his *Little Shepherd* (Cat. 38), an idyllic scene in which vigorous painting reflects the advanced techniques he had learned in Munich. Shirlaw's actual ties with Chicago terminated with his trip abroad, and he spent the rest of his career in the East. During his Chicago years, in the 1860s, Shirlaw was one of a large group of painters from that city who traveled during the summers to the Rocky Mountains, inspired by the success achieved by Albert Bierstadt with his trailblazing paintings of that region. Shirlaw had studied in Munich in 1870 with his Chicago colleague, James Farrington Gookins, who had also visited and painted the Rockies. Unlike Shirlaw, Gookins returned to Chicago to become one of the city's leading artists in the post-fire years, specializing in fairy paintings and landscapes, the latter drawn from both German and Colorado views, such as his *Western Landscape* (Cat. 42), painted in 1880.

Few Chicago landscape painters of the time, in fact, drew on local scenery; one of the leading specialists in the late nineteenth century, Daniel Folger Bigelow, derived material for his work on trips to Wisconsin and Lake Michigan, while also regularly journeying east to the Adirondacks and throughout New England. In *New England Landscape* (Cat. 27), he captured the prototypical charm of a quiet rural scene in the foothills of what may be the White or Green Mountains. Probably the leading local exponent of Barbizon-inspired landscape painting to draw his subject matter primarily from local scenery was Charles Francis Browne, whose *The Clearing* (Cat. 58) may have been painted in or around Oregon, Illinois, on the Rock River, the site of the best-known artists' colony in the state.[4] But other landscapists usually went even farther afield. Oliver Dennett Grover, celebrated for both his figure and landscape paintings, gained fame for his images of Venice, and in this country, ventured west to Glacier National Park in Montana, which he visited in the early 1920s, painting there his glowing *Avalanche Lake* (Cat. 54). Rudolphe Frank Ingerle headed in the opposite direction and became the leading painter in the Smoky Mountains of North Carolina; his *Oconolufty* [*sic*] (Cat. 3) is a scene at Oconaluftee in Cherokee, North Carolina. It is possible that Ingerle's activity in the Smokies attracted John Adams Spelman to the region, where he painted *North Carolina Mountains* (Cat. 56) of ca. 1926.

By the 1910s, the darker, more somber tones of French Barbizon-inspired landscapes, seen in the work of Bigelow, had been superseded by more vigorously painted and brightly colored scenes reflecting the influence of Impressionism. And a few landscape painters were beginning to find their subject matter regionally, if not in and around Chicago itself. Alfred Jansson, a specialist in seasonal landscapes, painted the colorful *Fall Landscape, Galena* (Cat. 59) at one of the state's earliest settlements of significance on the Mississippi River in the northwest corner of Illinois, while Frank Peyraud was active around Peoria, southwest of Chicago, where the farmland may have furnished the subject matter for his *October* (Cat. 18), which combines the drama and bold forms of Barbizon landscape painting with the color and light of Impressionism. Frank Virgil Dudley found his cherished theme in the dunes along the southern shore of Lake Michigan in nearby northern Indiana, which were, truly for him, *The Land of Song and Sky* (Cat. 5).[5] For the most part, however, Chicago landscape painters identified themselves with the artists' colonies that had sprung up throughout the nation. Of these, the leading community in the Midwest was in Nashville, in Brown County, Indiana, where Ingerle had previously painted and where Lucie Hartrath found her greatest inspiration. Hartrath was one of the leading women artists in both the colony and in Chicago. The appeal of the hilly, rural, and somewhat wild terrain of Brown County was not confined to summer visitors; Hartrath painted there in the autumn as well (Cat. 2), and it is possible that one or both of Karl Brandner's winter scenes in the Friedman Collection were rendered in Brown County, which he is known to have frequented (Cat. 39).[6] Perhaps the most celebrated of all the American artists' colonies was Old Lyme on the Connecticut coast, where

Wilson Henry Irvine painted his *Old Lyme Pond* (Cat. 57). He made Old Lyme his permanent home in 1918. Lawrence Mazzanovich had earlier settled in another Connecticut artists' colony in Westport, but he had studied in Chicago, and throughout much of his career continued a strong connection with the city through the Thurber Galleries there. The gallery promoted his softly rendered, tonal views of the rolling hills and coast of Connecticut, such as his *Moonlight at Dawn* (Cat. 29). A specific location is difficult to discern in Charles William Dahlgreen's *Frosty Morning* (Cat. 47), where the artist concentrated on the exploration of weather, light, color, shapes, and paint surface in an agricultural setting; the distant mountains are suggestive of the Ozarks of northern Arkansas or the Blue Ridge Mountains of North Carolina, two of the many areas where Dahlgreen painted, though he was also quite active in Brown County, Indiana.

The most celebrated colorist of all among the Chicago painters of the turn of the twentieth century was Norwegian-born Svend Svendsen who, like Jansson, was another immigrant from Scandinavia; indeed, the Swedish contribution to Chicago's cultural heritage beginning at the end of the nineteenth century can hardly be overestimated (Norway was united with Sweden until 1905). Svendsen developed a distinct combination of brilliant color and bright sunlight. Primarily a landscapist, his *Men Scything* (Cat. 6) is a rare figural example of his art. Brown County, Indiana, attracted not only Chicago landscape specialists such as Hartrath, but figure painters as well. One of the finest of these was Adam Emory Albright, who became one of the country's leading painters of rustic children in outdoor settings. Albright often used his twin sons as models, as in *Two Boys Fishing (Ivan and Malvin Albright)* (Cat. 55). As the boys grew older, Albright naturally turned to other juvenile models, as in *Children Playing on a Sandy Shore* (Cat. 41). Among Chicago's other leading figural painters of the early twentieth century were Pauline Palmer and Frederick Frary Fursman. Palmer's *Patsy* (Cat. 49) is an unusual, rather academically-rendered, tribute to feminine beauty and vanity by an artist more often involved with more Impressionist strategies. Fursman's work also consisted of outdoor imagery of women, rendered in an increasingly brilliant palette that, for a while at least, in works such as his *Woman in Blue Middy* (Cat. 51), veered beyond Impressionism in colorist intensity and vivacious brushwork; such paintings reflected his immersion in European Fauvism during a stay in Europe in 1913–14. Danish-born John C. Johansen studied in Chicago and painted there for a while, but in 1908 he moved to New York City, where he increasingly established a reputation as one of the finest portraitists of the period. His images consisted of both formal portrayals and even more appealing casual compositions with his sitters comfortably ensconced in their private environments, such as *The Collector* (Cat. 50), which depicts the president of the Metropolitan Museum of Art, Robert de Forest, and his wife.

The reputations of a number of early twentieth-century Chicago painters have been based primarily on the work they did abroad. George Ames Aldrich settled in Chicago at the end of World War I, but he had already made his reputation for paintings of gently flowing streams through villages in northeastern France, such as *Normandy River* (Cat. 30); here he emulated the work of the great Norwegian painter, Fritz Thaulow, which was extremely popular in the United States as well as in Europe. But it was the later generation of Americans who made up the artists' colony in Giverny, France, the home of Claude Monet, that reflected the closest ties with Chicago. In the early 1900s Frederick Frieseke, Lawton Parker, and Karl Anderson had all studied at the Art Institute of Chicago before going abroad and painting in Giverny, followed by Karl Buehr and Louis Ritman, both represented in the Friedman Collection.[7] The primary subject of all these artists were lovely women, often in outdoor floral settings. Therefore, Buehr's *The North Country (Haystacks)* (Cat. 46) is an unusual work in the artist's oeuvre, depicting a farm landscape that reflects the agrarian economy of the village while portraying its well-known sloping hillside in the background. Buehr settled in Giverny in 1909, and therefore would have had the opportunity of knowing both Theodore Earl Butler and Lilla Cabot Perry. Butler was an essential American expatriate. Having married not one, but two of Monet's stepdaughters, he was a conduit between the great French Impressionist and the American colonists, though few of the latter ever became close with Monet. Butler himself, from Columbus, Ohio, painted in a modified Impressionist manner informed by more Post-Impressionist trends, seen equally in figural works and pure landscapes, such as his *Valley Farm* (*Cottage in Giverny*) (Cat. 31).

Boston's Lilla Cabot Perry spent nine non-successive seasons in Giverny, the last in 1909, corresponding to Buehr's first appearance there. Perry had become one of the few Americans who did establish a close friendship with Monet, writing an important essay on the great French artist shortly after his death in 1926. *The Poacher* (Cat. 19), one of her finest and most monumental figure paintings, combines strong structure with the color, light, and broken brushwork of Impressionism, especially noticeable in the expansive landscape behind the figure. Ritman arrived in Giverny in 1911, too late to meet Perry there, but unlike Buehr he was one of the few colonists to remain during World War I, and he continued to paint in Giverny and in Paris during the decades that followed, though his work was regularly exhibited back in Chicago. The three examples in the Friedman collection, all devoted to female imagery, explore his diverse thematic concerns. *Jean* (cat. 28) portrays an attractive young woman, elegantly dressed and posed against a decorative floral-patterned background. *René* (Cat. 25) is a study of the partial nude, a subject painted by many of this generation of American artists in Giverny. And *At the Piano* (Cat. 48) is a domestic interior, seemingly more "slice of life" than a posed figural study, with the young woman's face deliberately hidden from the viewer.

Perhaps the most distinctive component of the Friedman Collection is the large and diverse group of pictures of, and relating to, the city itself. "Cityscapes," as such, were not common in American art until the last decade and a half of the nineteenth century, when the painting of city scenes—streets, buildings, and urban parks—began to be undertaken by American painters primarily in New York and, to some extent Boston, by artists working in both the Impressionist and Tonalist aesthetic. This first generation of artists of the urban scene pretty much passed Chicago by, which is curious, given Chicago's importance in the development of modern architecture. It was only about 1910 that pictorial interest in rendering the great city really began to develop, echoing the literary concerns for urban subjects found in the writing of Theodore Dreiser and Carl Sandburg.[8] Almost certainly, the artists were responding to the concept of "The New Chicago," as discussed by another of the leading authors of the city, Hamlin Garland.[9]

Occasionally painters, such as Frank T. Moore Beatty, here with his *LaSalle Street* (Cat. 53), emulated earlier New York artists such as Childe Hassam and Colin Campbell Cooper in painting tall skyscrapers and urban "canyons."[10] More often, Chicago artists were drawn to the industrial landscape and especially to the Chicago River, as in James Jeffrey Grant's outstanding urban view, *Michigan Avenue Bridge* (Cat. 1), in which he contrasted monumental vertical architecture with the busy horizontals of street and bridge traffic over the waterway.

One of the earliest such images of Chicago, unusual for an artist primarily associated with rural subject matter, is by the Impressionist painter, Charles William Dahlgreen. In his *Rush Street Bridge* of ca. 1910 (Cat. 9), the artist's typical colorful palette and fluid brushwork animate the dynamics of an industrial river scene. More somber are the muted tones that define the industrial waterway, which became a specialty of Torey Ross, still another Swedish-born Chicago artist, as in his *Watertanks, Chicago River* (Cat. 8), and his nocturnal *Chicago River at Night* (Cat. 35). The river is also the setting for some works. George Schultz, primarily a painter of sea and river scenes, featured old utilitarian working vessels in *Chicago River* (Cat. 14), while in Swedish-born Gerda Ahlm's *Fishing in Chicago* (Cat. 33), the focus is on small pleasure boats, with the city and bridge in the background.

One of the best-studied of the Chicago's painters was Dutch-born Tunis Ponsen, whose urban depictions covered a full strata from skyline, riverscapes, and industrial scenes to local neighborhoods such as that portrayed in *Winter Streets, Chicago* (Cat. 32).[11] Ponsen's urban scenes usually include figures, strolling or working, and in some, such as his *Repair Gang* (Cat. 36), the emphasis is on toiling human activity rather than on city streets. A more densely crowded world of urban workers and shoppers—the majority obviously women—appear in a view of a corner of *State Street* (Cat. 52) by Ruth Van Sickle Ford, a picture especially close in spirit to the earlier work of New York's Ashcan School.[12] Urban leisure areas as well as industrial locations attracted these Chicago painters. Torey Ross, for instance, suggested a brilliantly lit pleasure garden beyond the river in his nocturnal vista portrayed in *Riverview Park* (Cat. 20). Frederic Milton Grant celebrated Chicago's *Century of Progress Exposition* of 1933–34 in *Entrance to Western Union Hall, Century of Progress International Exposition, Chicago* (Cat. 60). This vibrant work portrays fair-goers milling around before the entrance to one of the exposition's three "Electrical Buildings." Western Union Hall was embellished with a high relief sculpture, inscribed "The Conquest of Time and Space," and it was here that a century of telegraphic history was on display. Indeed, the picture, with its yellow facade, reflects the fair's objective, stated by one of its commissioners, to stand as a symbol of the architecture of the future, its bold and colorful buildings sustaining the modern movement.[13] A sophisticated populace enjoying boating at one of the favorite summer retreats of wealthy Chicagoans at Lake Geneva, Wisconsin is portrayed, in *Holiday (Lake Geneva)* (Cat. 10), painted by Carl R. Krafft, otherwise a landscape specialist active both in the Ozarks with Ingerle and in Brown County. A similar spirit pervades Minnie Harms Neebe's *Oak Street Beach* (Cat. 17), which depicts the local populace—women and children (suggesting a weekday scene where the males would be at work)—engaging in the commonplace pleasures of sunbathing, swimming, and boating. Indeed, Lake Michigan itself attracted local painters. Norwegian-born John Olson Hammerstad painted several sailing vessels far out on rough seas under a brilliant sunset sky in his *Lake Michigan* of 1887 (Cat. 11), but a different, more cheerful spirit prevails in Harold Betts's calm panorama of small pleasure craft in *Clouds Forming over Lake Michigan* of 1917 (Cat. 40). In all these paintings, Chicago artists of the first half of the twentieth century were forging their distinct identities in defining their explicit environment.

William H. Gerdts
Professor Emeritus of Art History
Graduate School of the City University of New York

---

1. To date the most important publications surveying Chicago art are: Esther Sparks, *A Biographical Dictionary of Painters and Sculptors in Illinois, 1808–1845*, Ph. D. diss., Northwestern University, Evanston, Ill., 1971; and William H. Gerdts, *Art Across America: Two Centuries of Regional Painting*, 3 vols. (New York: Abbeville Press, 1990), vol. 2, pp. 285–322.

2. See the brochure by Susan C. Larsen, Wendy Greenhouse, and Susan S. Weininger, *Chicago Painting 1895 to 1945: The Bridges Collection* (Springfield, Ill., Illinois State Museum, 2000). The catalogue accompanying this exhibition is still anticipated

3.   Kenneth Robert Hey, *Five Artists and the Chicago Modernist Movement, 1909–1928*. Ph.D. diss., Emory University, Atlanta, Ga. 1973; *The Emergence of Modernism in Illinois, 1914–1940* (Springfield, Ill., Illinois State Museum, 1976); Sue Ann Prince, *The Old Guard and the Avant-Garde: Modernism in Chicago, 1910–1940* (Chicago: University of Chicago Press, 1990); Susan Weininger, *Thinking Modern: Painting in Chicago 1910–1940* (Evanston, Ill.: Mary and Leigh Block Gallery, Northwestern University, 1992). In the more specialized exhibition catalogue by Susan Weininger, *The "New Woman" in Chicago, 1910–1945: Paintings from Illinois Collections* (Rockford, Ill.: Rockford College in association with Illinois State Museum, Springfield, 1993)—only two of the artists in the Friedman collection, Ruth Van Sickle Ford and Minnie Harms Neebe, were represented. Minnie Neebe is the only artist of the first half of the twentieth century who is discussed in the survey by J. Z. Jacobson, *Art of Today Chicago—1933* (Chicago: L. M. Stein, 1932).

4.   Horace Spencer Fiske, "The Eagle's Nest," *Brush and Pencil* 2 (September 1898), pp. 271–5; Harriet Monroe, "Eagle's Nest Camps: A Colony of Artists and Writers," *House Beautiful* 16 (August 1904), pp. 5–10; Josephine Craven Chandler, "Eagle's Nest Camp, Barbizon of Chicago Artists," *Art and Archaeology* 12 (November 1921), pp. 194–204; Athalae Elliott McGuire, "Eagle's Nest Association, 1898–1942," Master's thesis, Northern Illinois University, DeKalb, 1964; Evelyn R. Moore, "Eagle's Nest Artist Colony, 1898–1942," *Historic Illinois* 7 (August 1984), pp. 2–3, 5; Timothy J. Garvey, "The Artist Is Out: Recreations of the 'Little Room' and 'Eagle's Nest'," *Selected Papers in Illinois History, 1984–1985* (Springfield, Ill.: Springfield Historical Society, 1987), pp. 59–67.

5.   The dune landscape is of special concern to the Westchester Township Historical Museum in Chesterton, Indiana, which is a service of the Westchester Public Library in cooperation with the Duneland Historical Society. Also in Chesterton is the Dunes National Lakeshore. See: Earl H. Reed, "The Sand Dunes," *Art, A Monthly Journal for Art Lovers* [O'Brien's Gallery, Chicago] 1 (January 1913), pp. 1–2; A. G. Richards, "Lake Michigan's Wonderful Dunes," *Fine Arts Journal*, 36 (June, 1918), pp. 19–25.

6.   Lyn Letsinger-Miller, *The Artists of Brown County* (Bloomington, Ind.: Indiana University Press, 1994), concentrates primarily on Indiana artists. A more encompassing survey, including a number of these Chicago painters, can be found in M. Joanne Nesbit, ed. and Barbara Judd, compiler, *These Brown County Artists: The Ones Who Came, The Ones Who Stayed, The Ones Who Moved On 1900–1950* (Nashville, Ind., Nana's Books, 1993).

7.   See William H. Gerdts, *Monet's Giverny: An Impressionist Colony* (New York: Abbeville Press, 1993), pp. 157–210.

8.   On Chicago cityscapes, see the important article by Wendy Greenhouse, "Picturing the City: Chicago Artists and the Urban Theme," *Block Points* 3–4 (1996/1998), pp. 76–97; and *Chicago: The Modernist Vision—Chicago Artists Paint Their City, 1920–1950* (Chicago: Robert Henry Adams Fine Art, 1990). Given the more traditional nature of the Friedman Collection, none of the painters illustrated and discussed in these publications are represented in it, except for George Ames Aldrich whose atypical *Steel* is reproduced in Greenhouse, p. 85. Greenhouse discusses the rise of unpicturesque urban imagery of Chicago in Wendy Greenhouse and Susan S. Weininger, *A Rediscovered Regionalist Herman Menzel* (Chicago Historical Society, 1994), and reproduces Torey Ross's *Houseboats and Watertanks* from the Friedman collection, pp. 18–19.

9.   Hamlin Garland, "The New Chicago," *Craftsman* 24 (September 1913), pp. 555–65.

10.   Other painters of the city's tall buildings and majestic skyline include more traditional artists such as Frederick Tellender and Richard Chase and modernists such as Todros Geller, William R. Schwartz, and Raymond Jonson; see Greenhouse, pp. 85–95.

11.   In the essays by William H. Gerdts and Susan S. Weininger in *The Lost Paintings of Tunis Ponsen (1891–1968)* (Muskegon, Mich., Muskegon Museum of Art, 1994), urban imagery by numerous other Chicago painters, including Jean Crawford Adams, Anthony Angarola, Emil Armin, Belle Baranceanu, Richard Chase, Todros Geller, Raymond Jonson, and Ramon Shiva offer further evidence of the vitality of the pictorial tradition that had developed in the city.

12.   Ford's *State Street* was included in the exhibition, *Paintings of Chicago by Chicago Artists* (Chicago: Art Institute of Chicago, 1937); James Jeffrey Grant was also represented in this show with *The Bridge in Winter* (very possibly, now, *Michigan Avenue Bridge*), in the Friedman Collection.

13.   John E. Findling, ed., *Historical Dictionary of World's Fairs and Expositions, 1851–1988* (New York: Greenwood Press, 1990, pp. 268, 273).

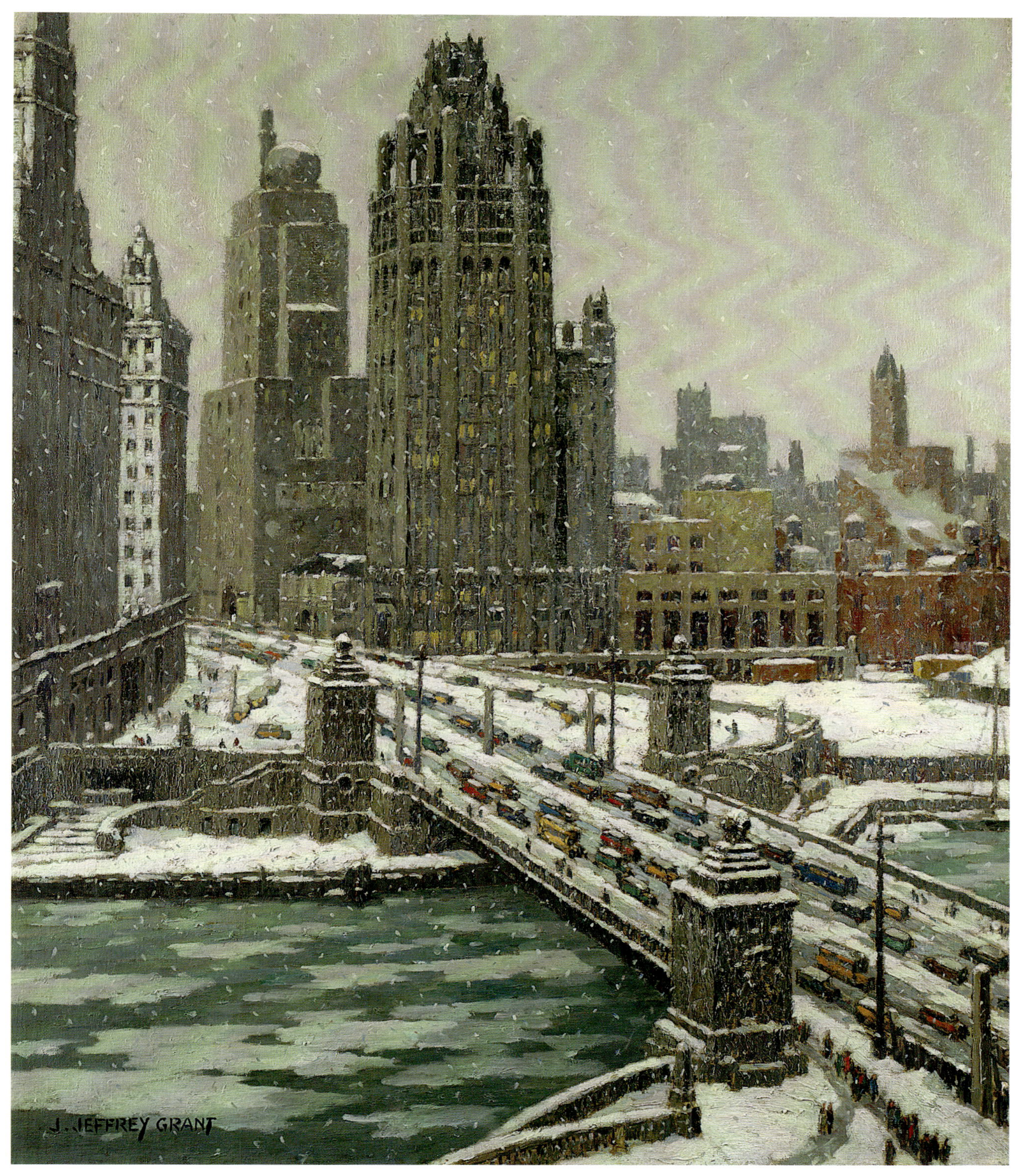

1. **James Jeffrey Grant** (1883–1960)
Michigan Avenue Bridge, 1925, oil on canvas, 35 × 30 inches

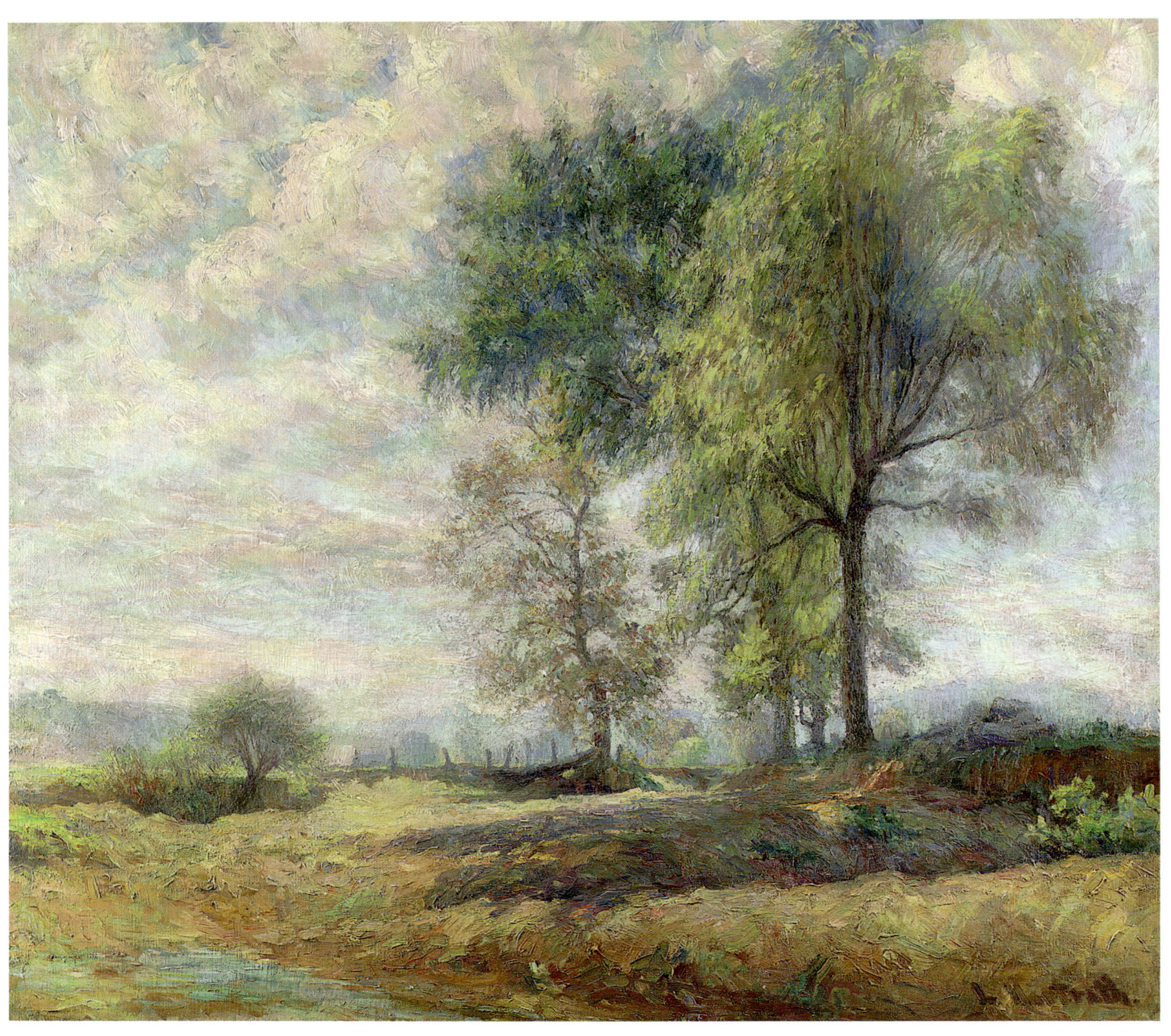

2. **Lucie Hartrath** (1867–1962)
Brown County Landscape, ca. 1916, oil on canvas, 36 × 40 inches

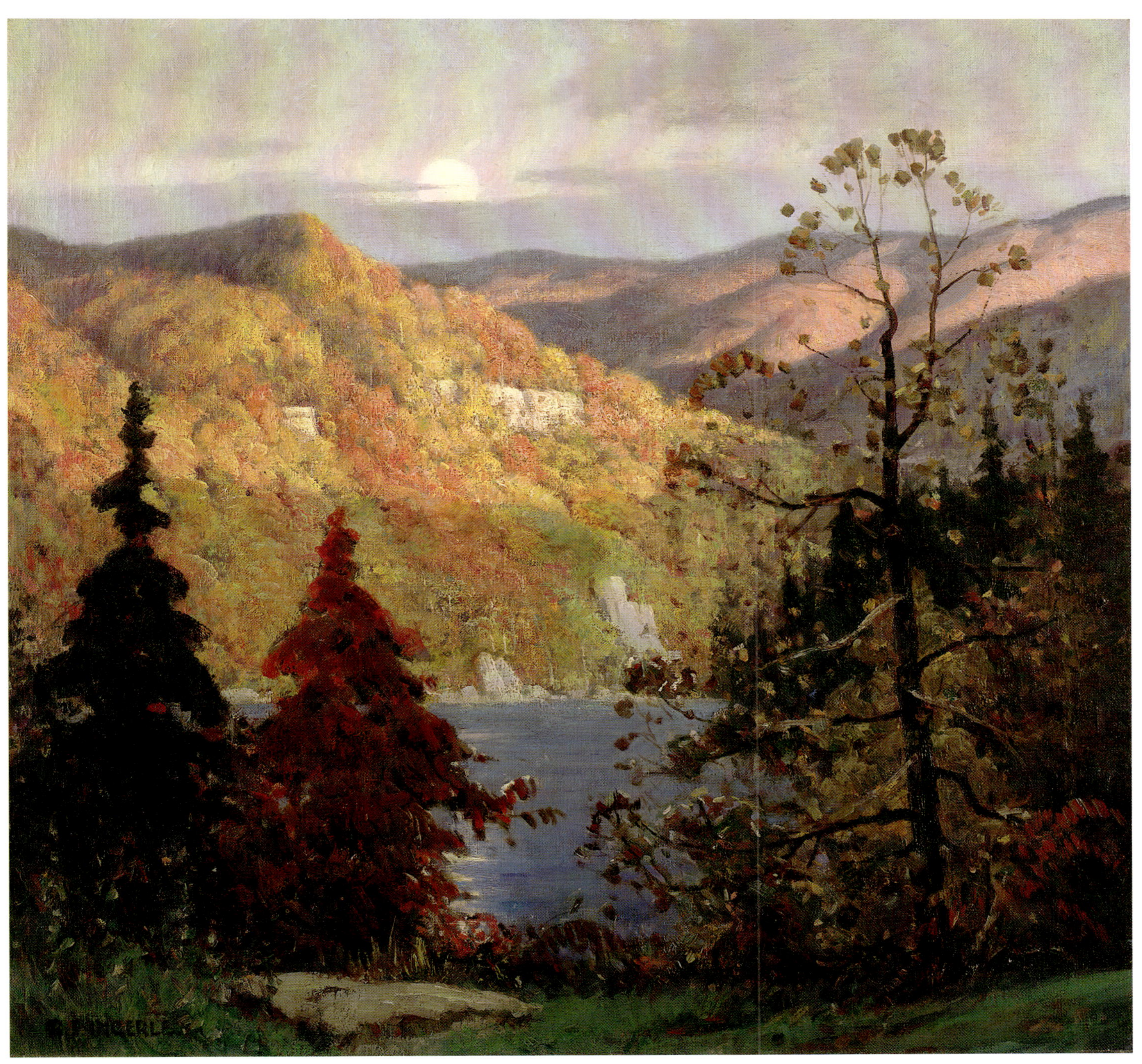

3. **Rudolph Frank Ingerle** (1879–1950)
Oconolufty [*sic*], ca. 1920, oil on board, 30 × 32 inches

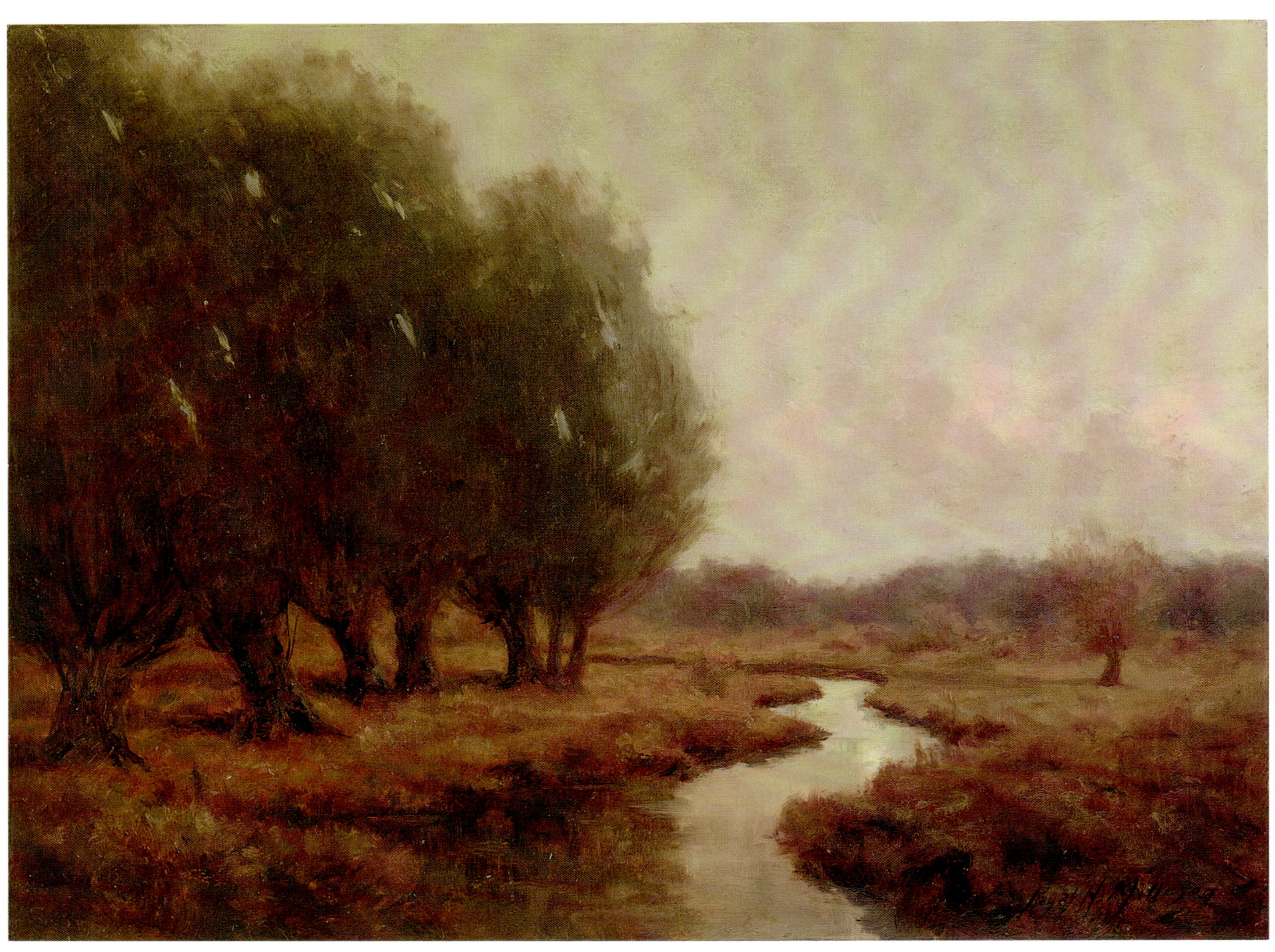

4. **Royal Hill Milleson** (1849–1935)
Landscape with Stream (Evening Landscape), ca. 1890, oil on canvas, 18 × 24 inches

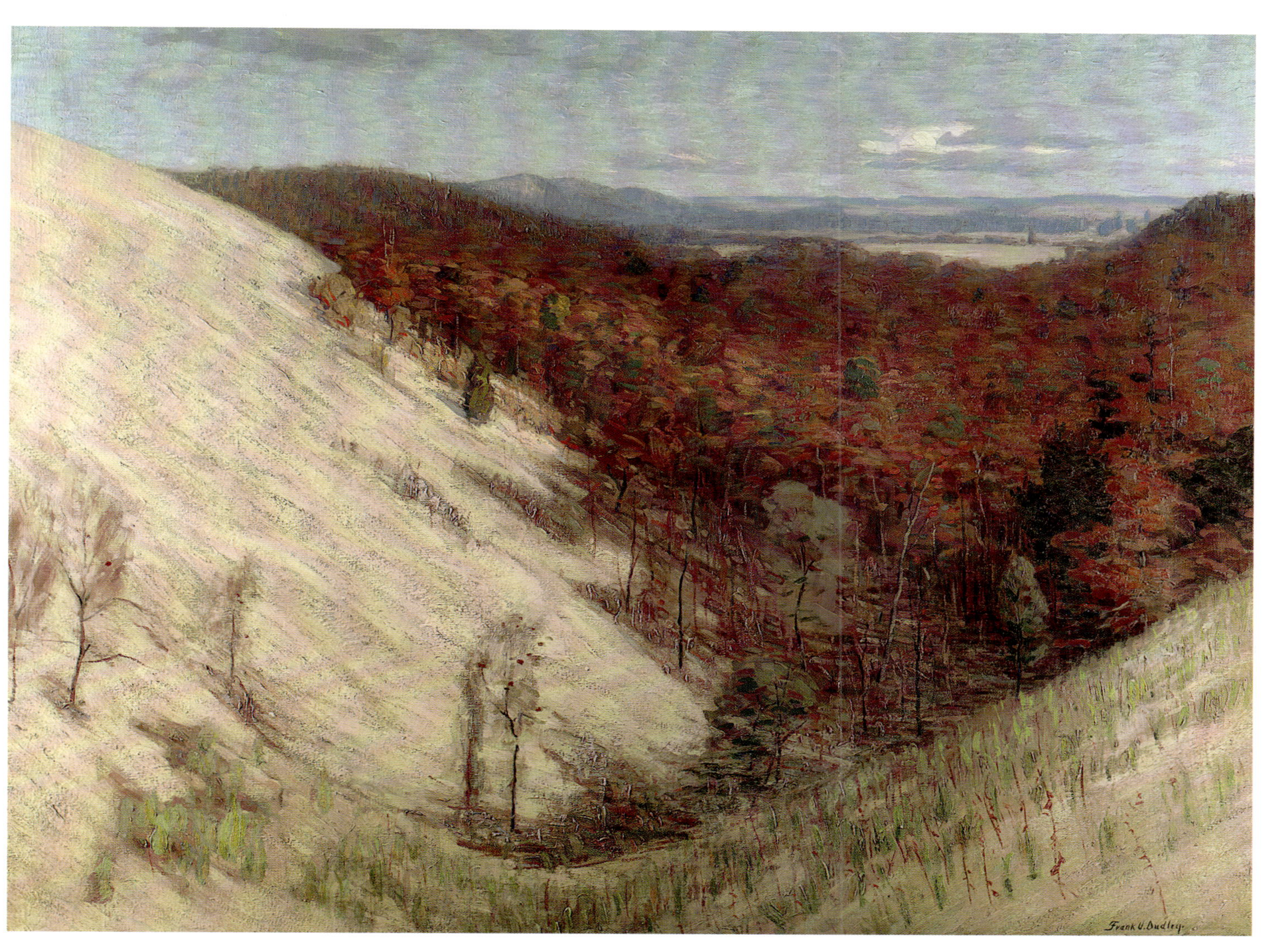

5. **Frank Virgil Dudley** (1868–1957)
The Land of Song and Sky, ca. 1918, oil on canvas, 44½ × 60 inches

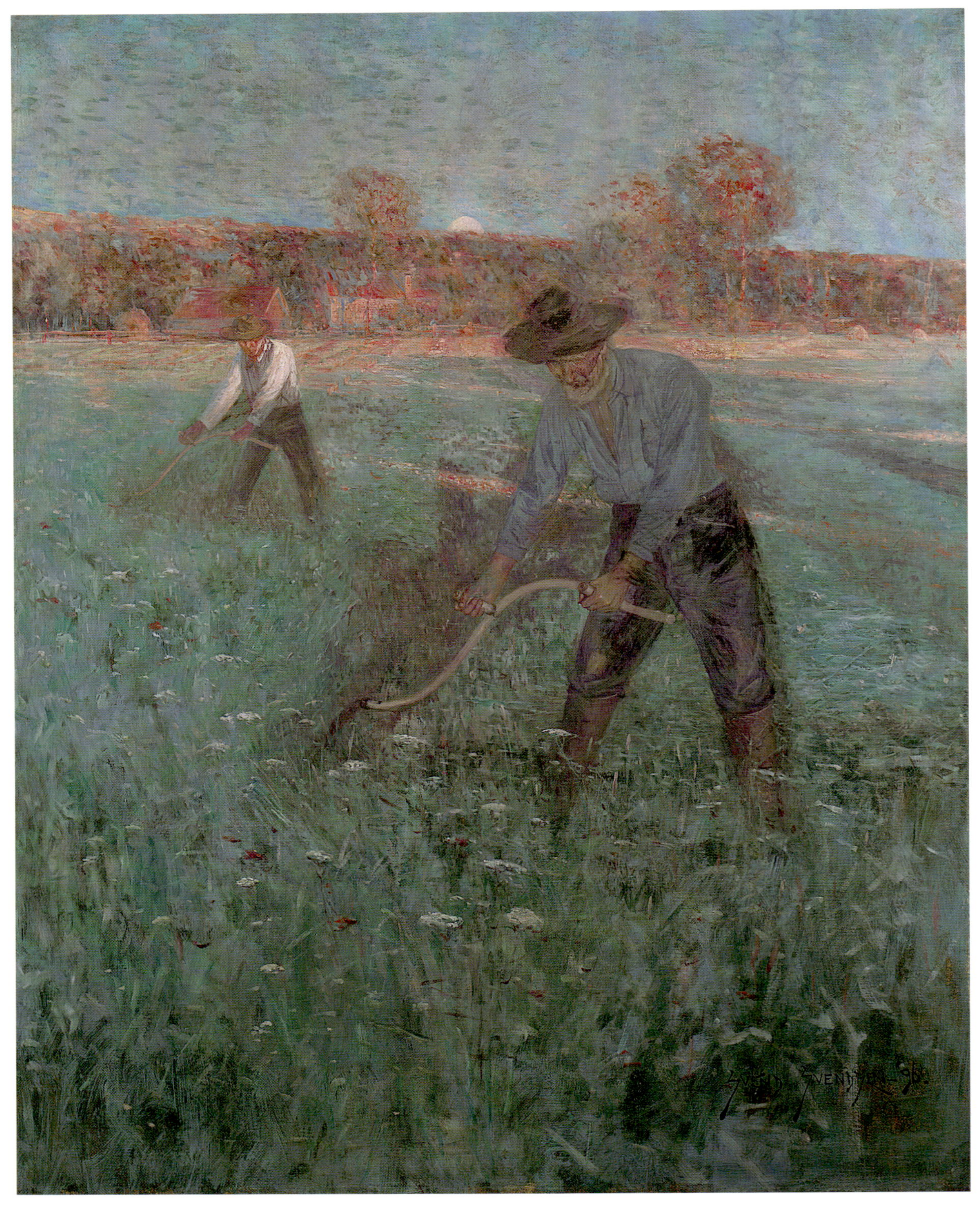

6. **Svend Svendsen** (1864–1945)
Men Scything, 1896, oil on canvas, 48 × 38 inches

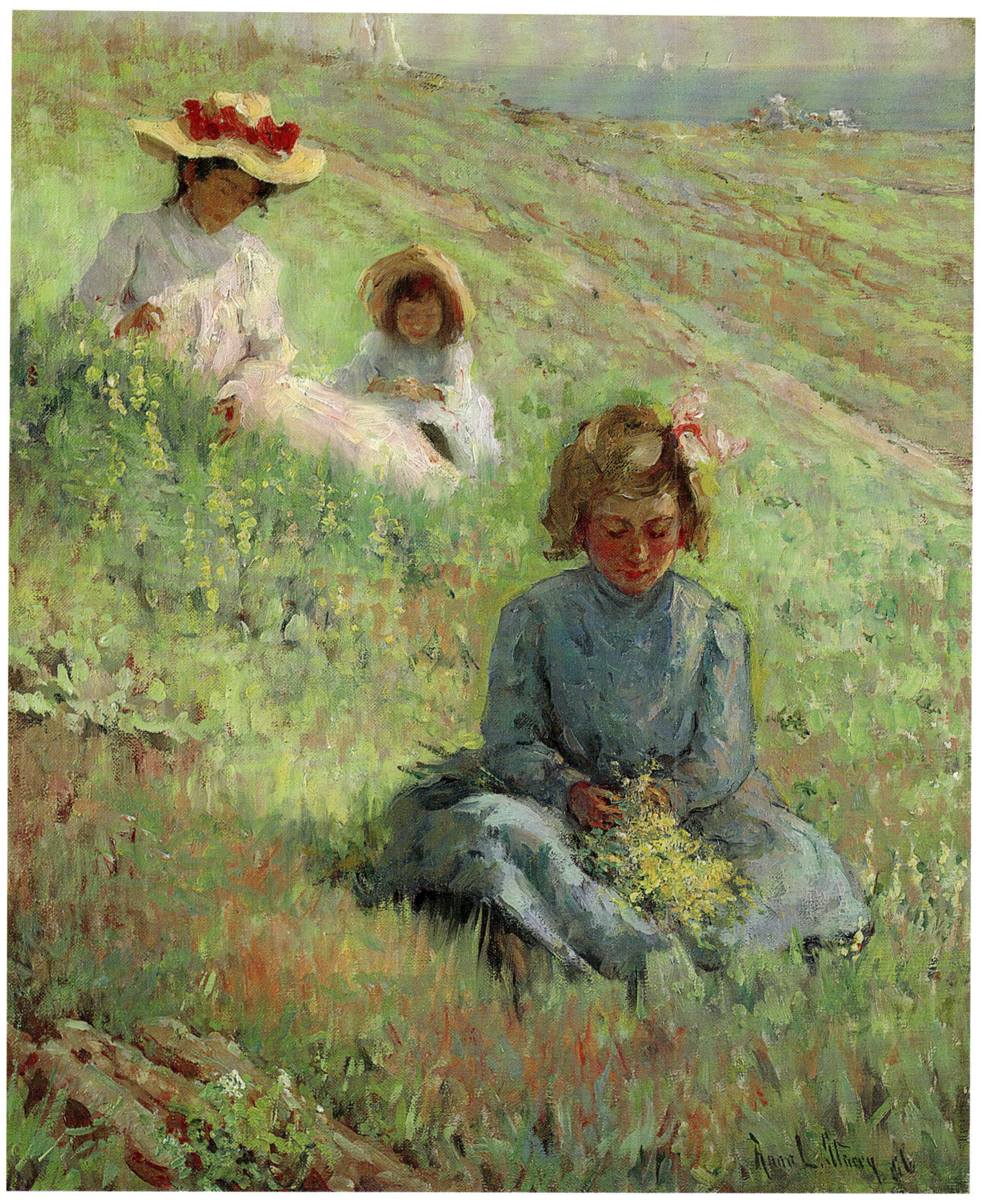

7. **Anna Lee Stacey** (1871–1943)
September on the Hillside, 1906, oil on canvas, 20 × 16 inches

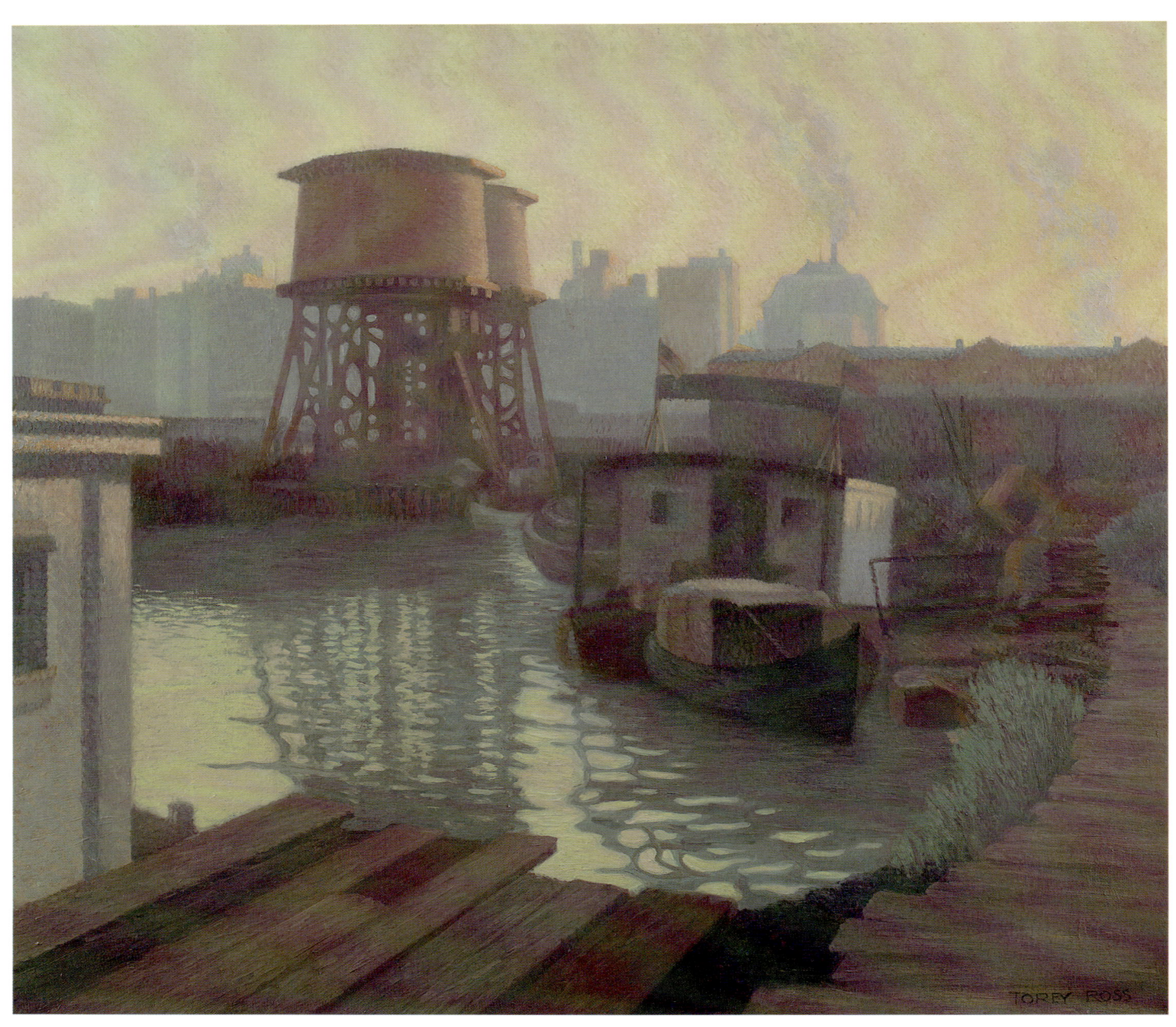

8. **Torey Ross** (1875–1966)
Watertanks, Chicago River, ca. 1927, oil on board, 28 × 34 inches

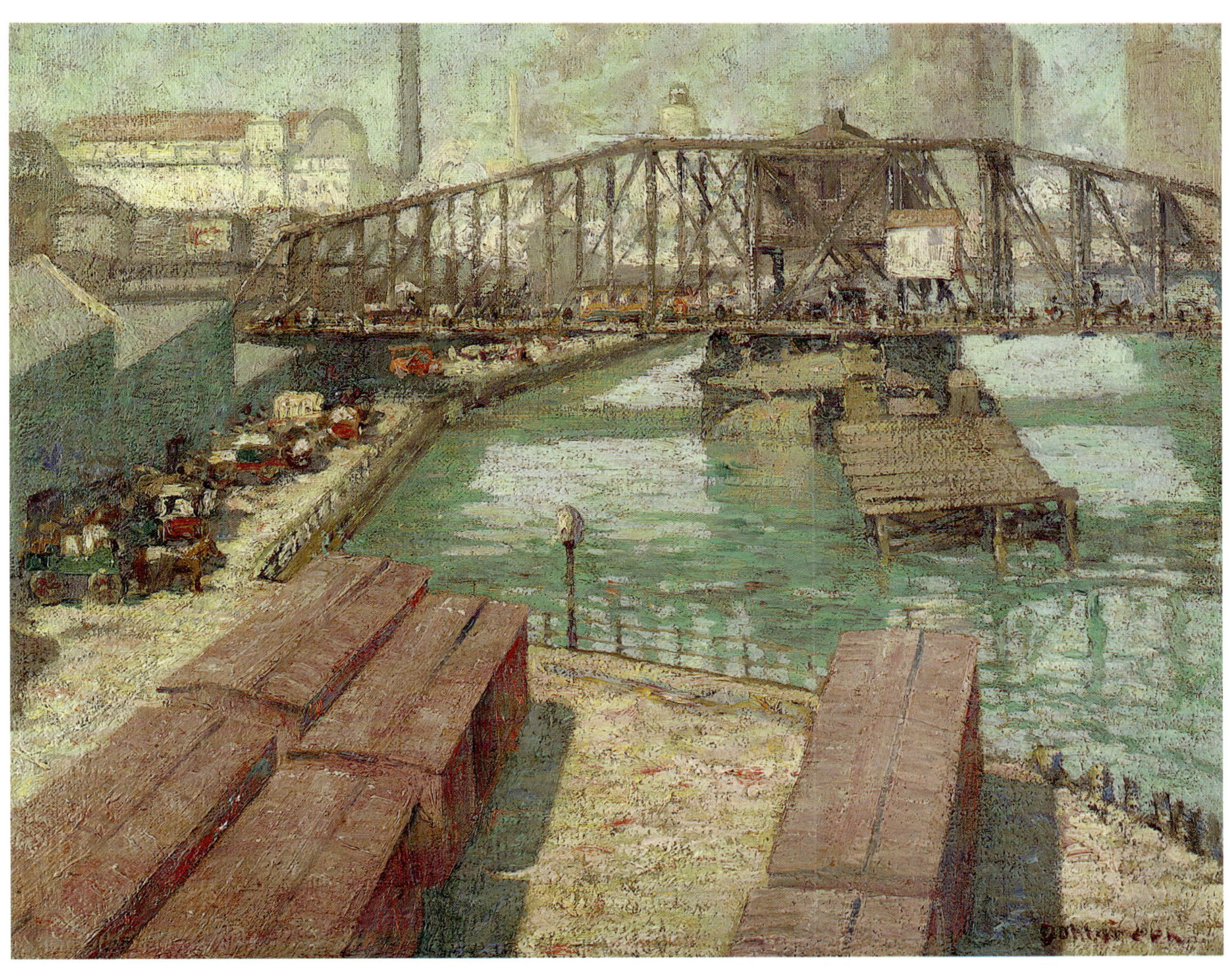

9. **Charles William Dahlgreen** (1864–1955)
Rush Street Bridge, ca. 1910, oil on canvas, 20 × 26 inches

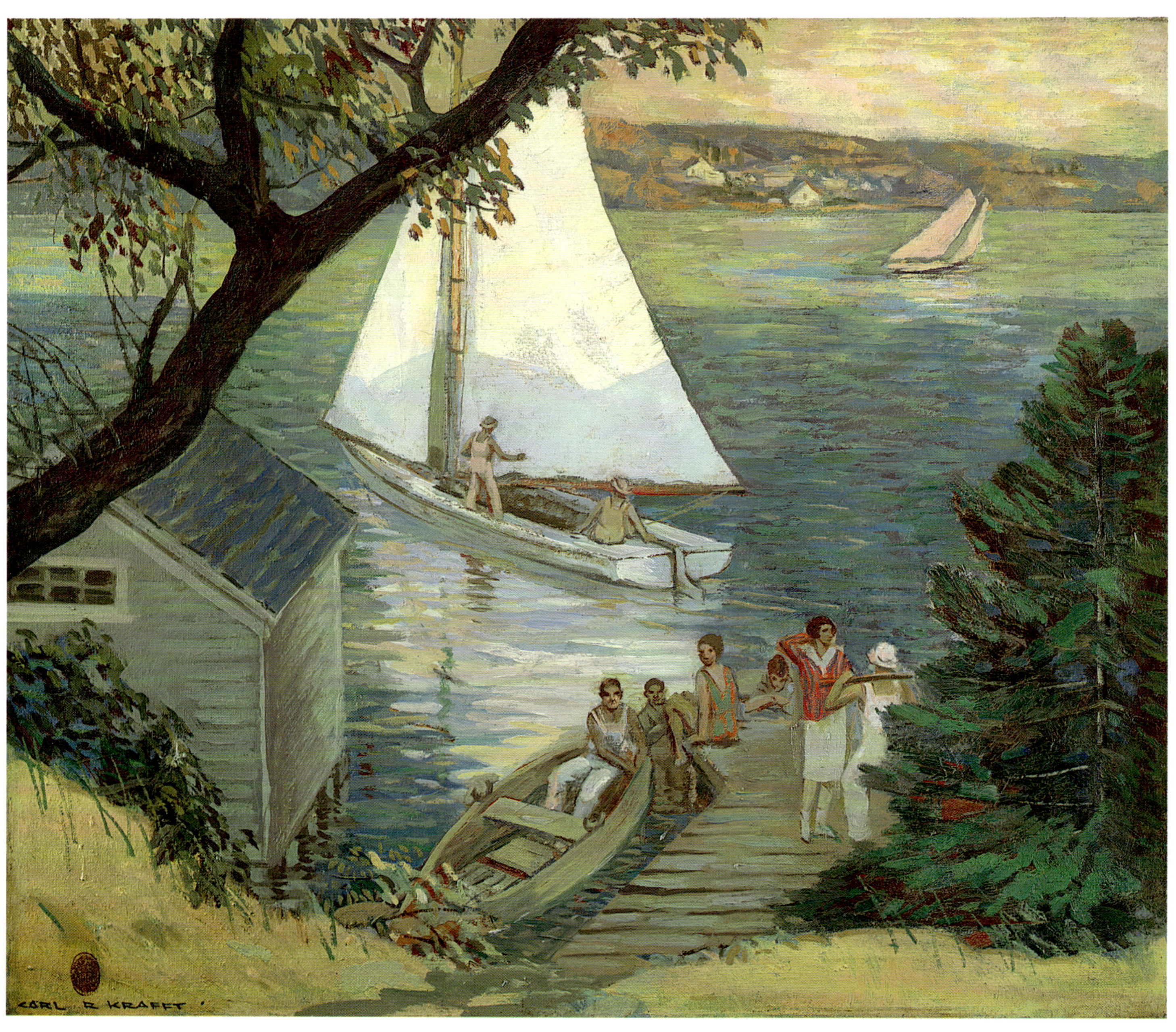

10. **Carl R. Krafft** (1884–1938)
Holiday (Lake Geneva), ca. 1925, oil on canvas, 24 × 27 inches

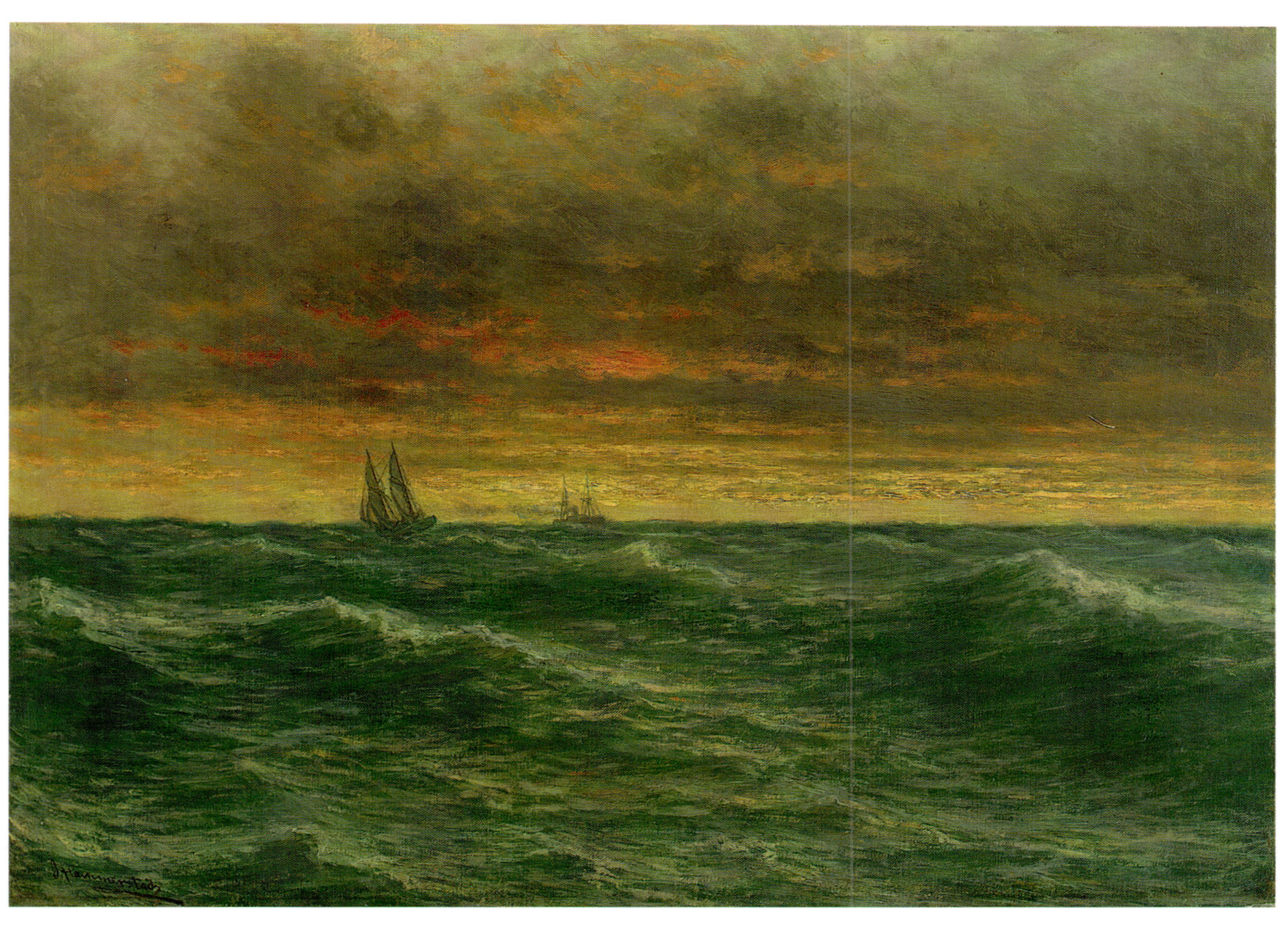

11. **John Olson Hammerstad** (1842–1925)
Lake Michigan, ca. 1887, oil on canvas, 20 × 28 inches

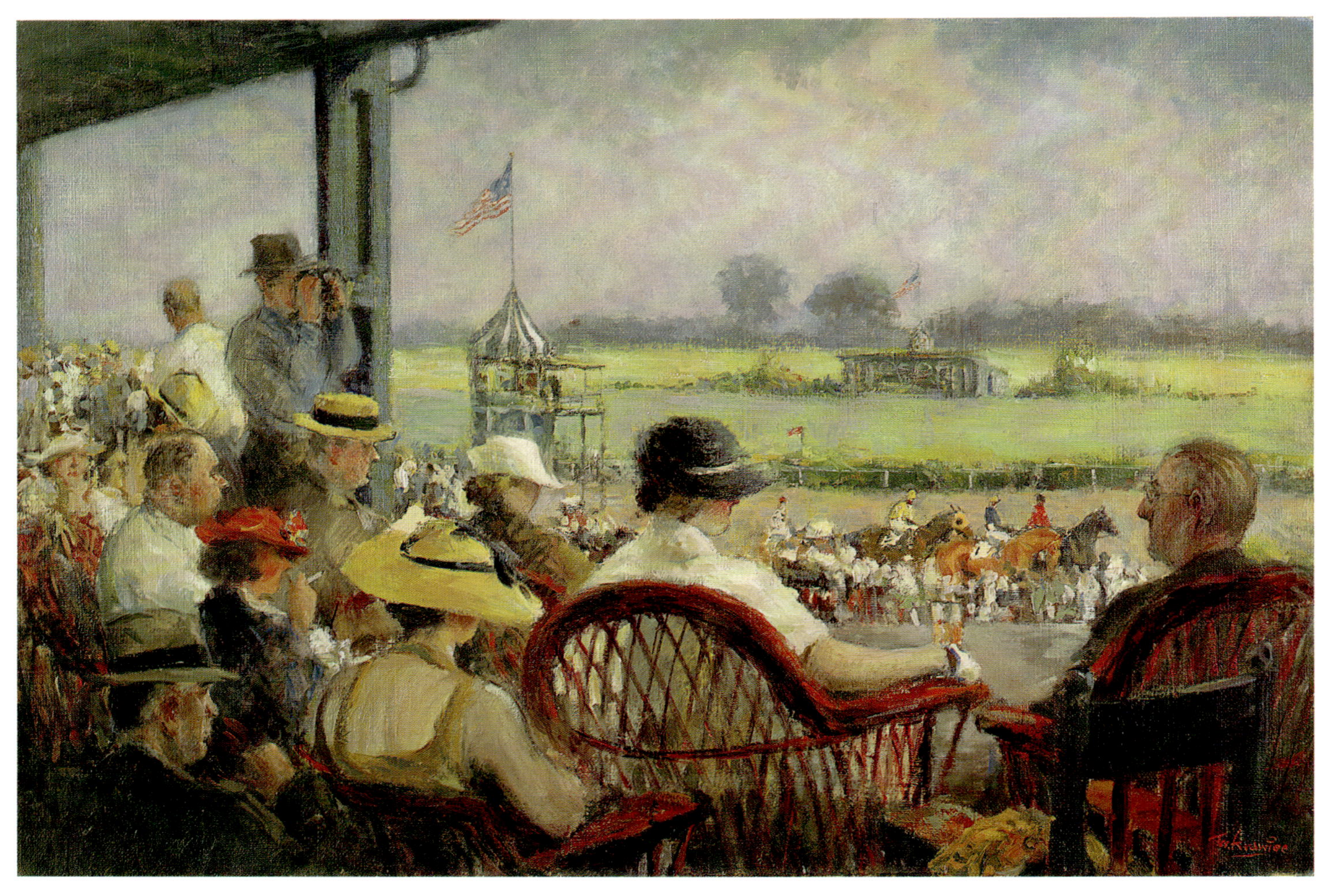

12. **Walter Krawiec** (1889–1982)
Post Time, ca. 1940, oil on canvas, 22 × 32 inches

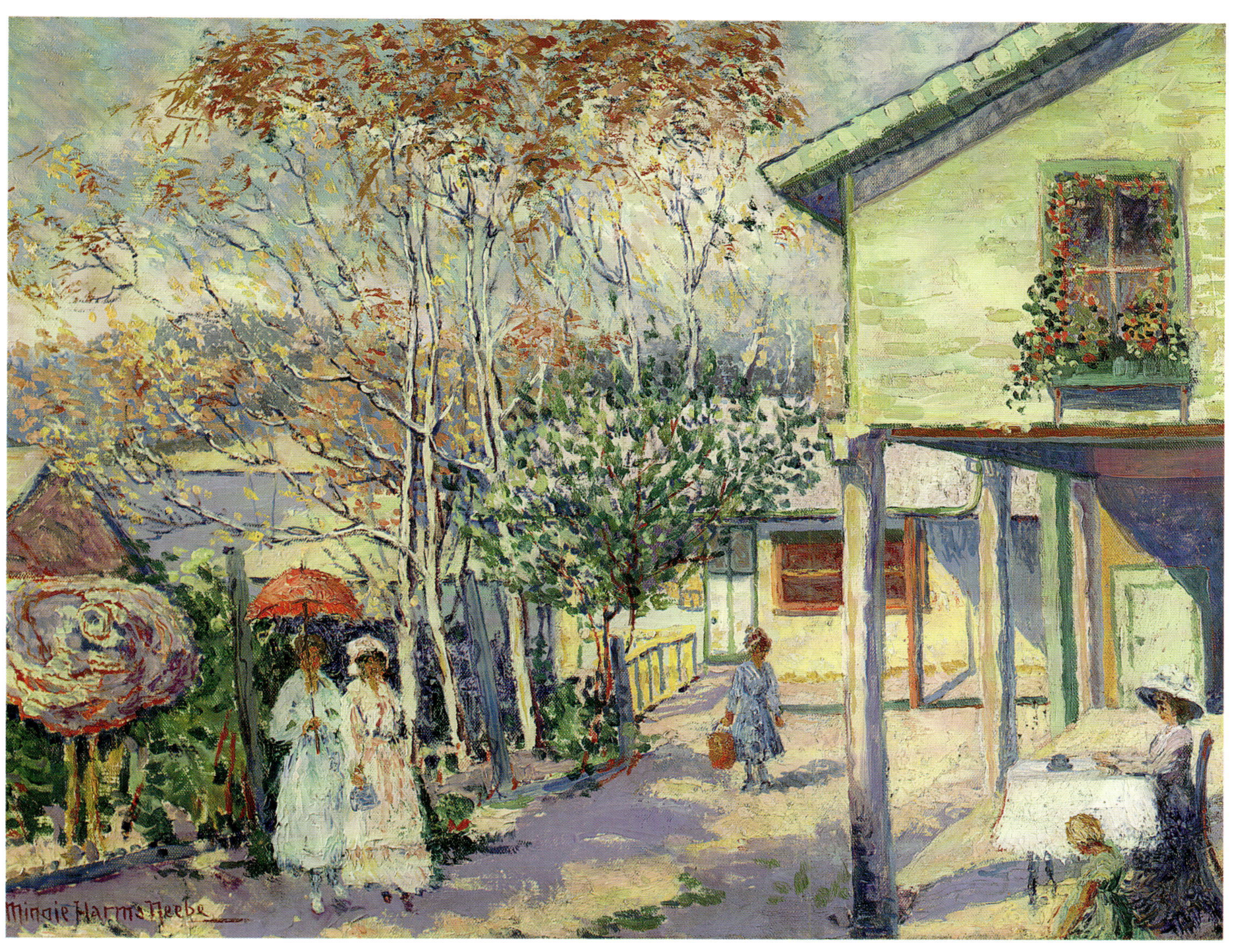

13. **Minnie Harms Neebe** (1873–1936)
Tea Time (Saugatuck, Michigan), ca. 1914, oil on canvas, 22¼ × 28¾ inches

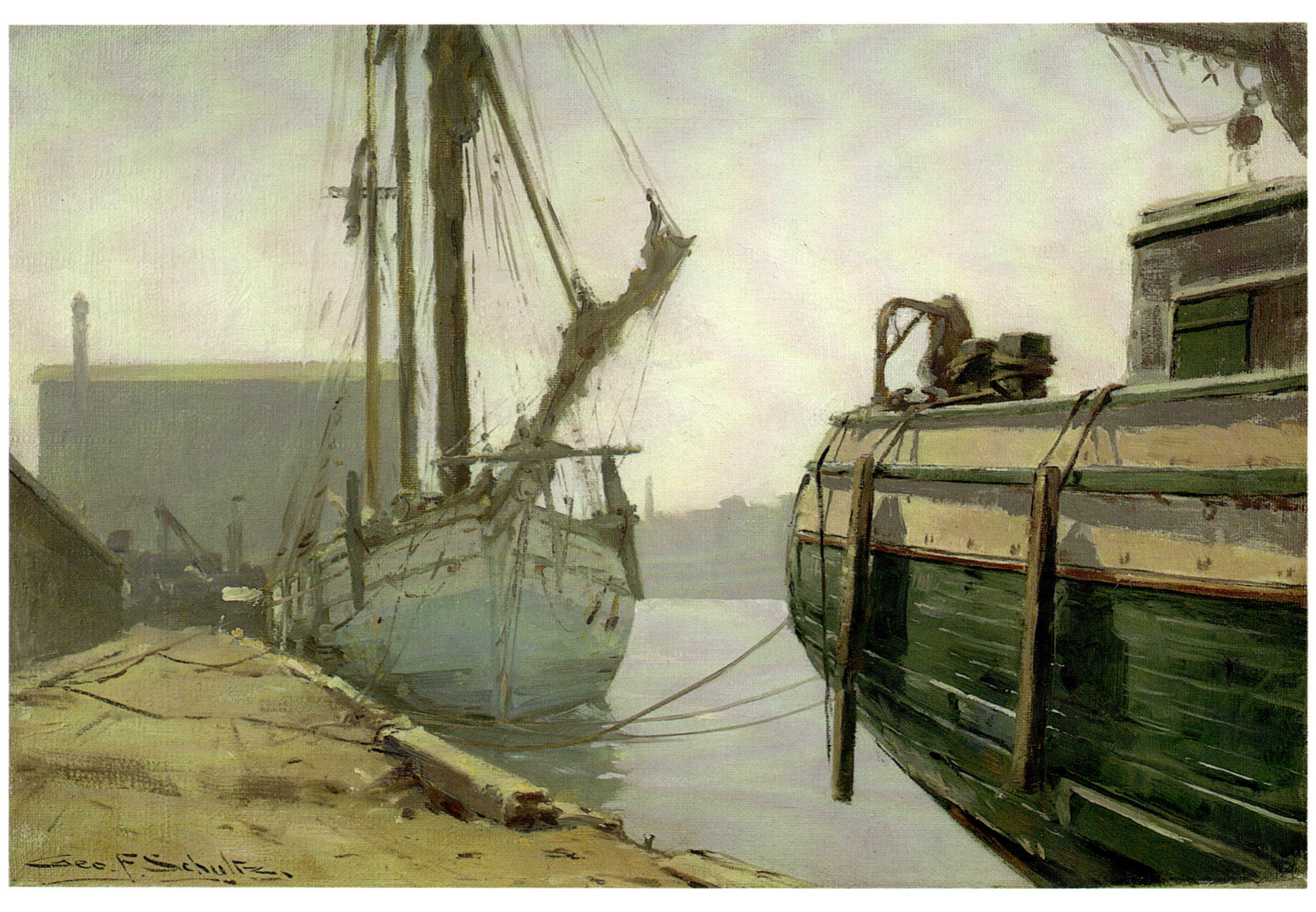

14. **George F. Schultz** (1869–1950)
Chicago River, ca. 1920, oil on canvas, 15 × 23 inches

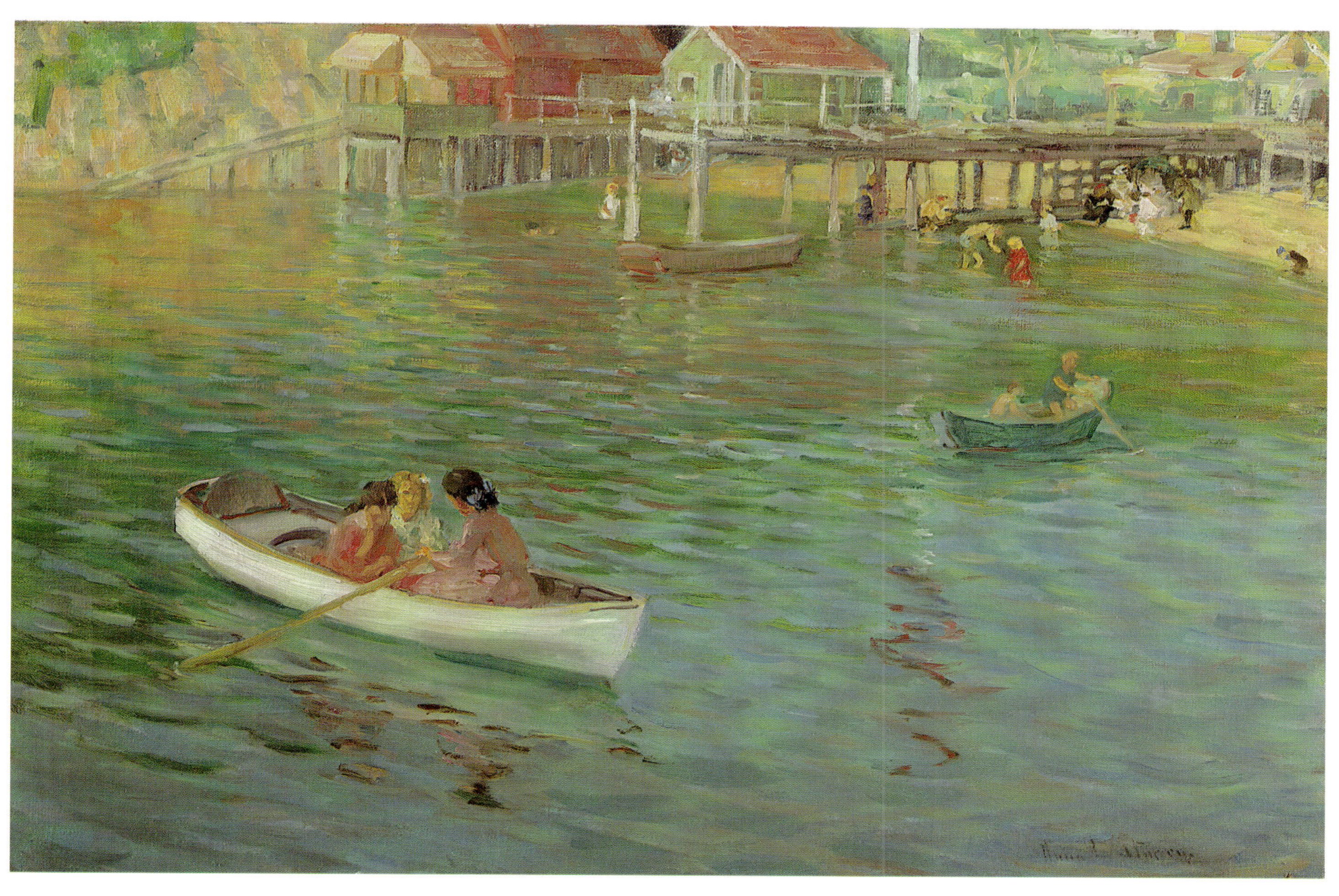

15. **Anna Lee Stacey** (1871–1943)
Women with Children Boating, ca. 1920, oil on canvas, 18 × 24 inches

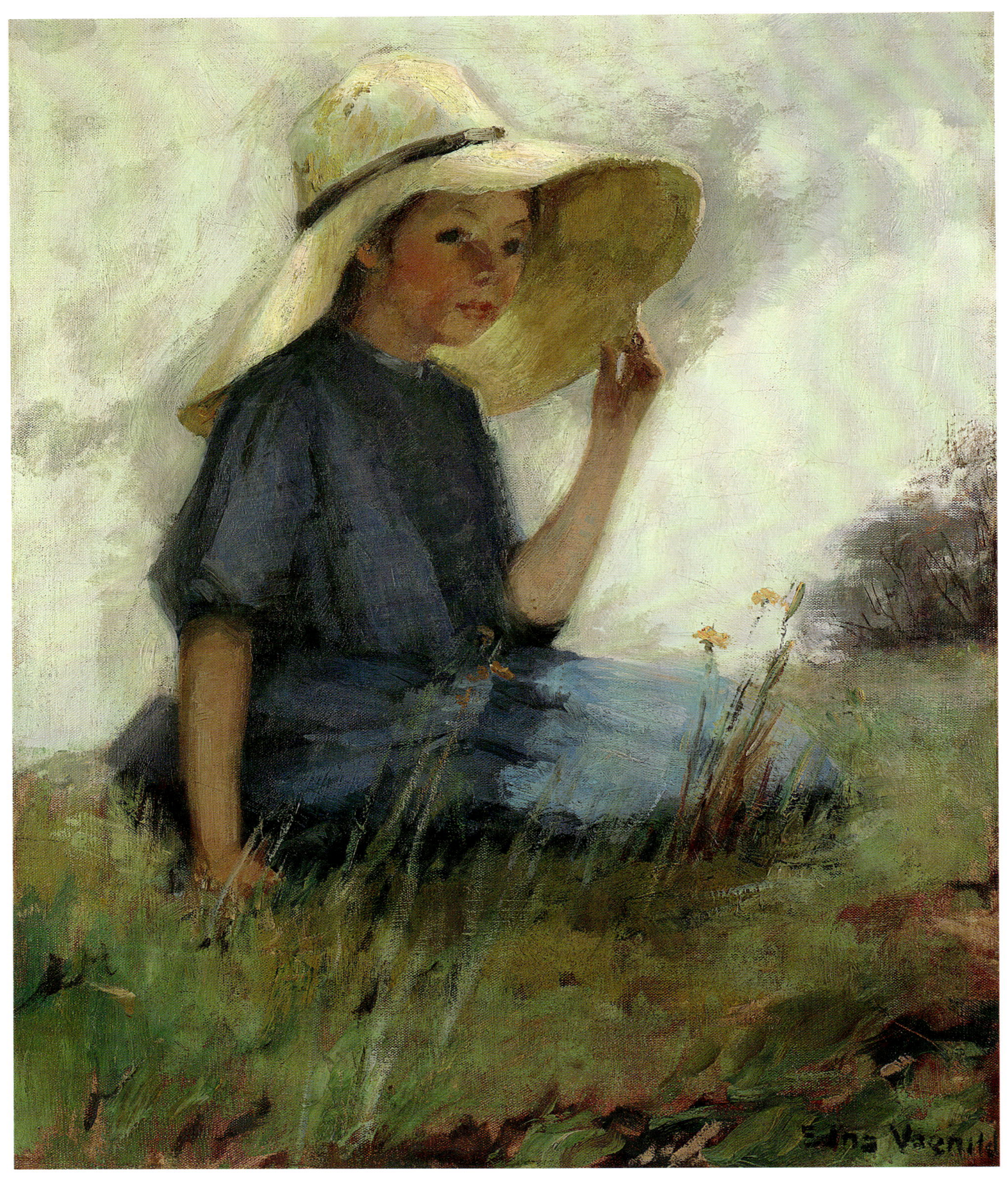

16. **Edna Vognild** (1877–1961)
Young Girl in a Floppy Hat, ca. 1908, oil on canvas, 28 × 24 inches

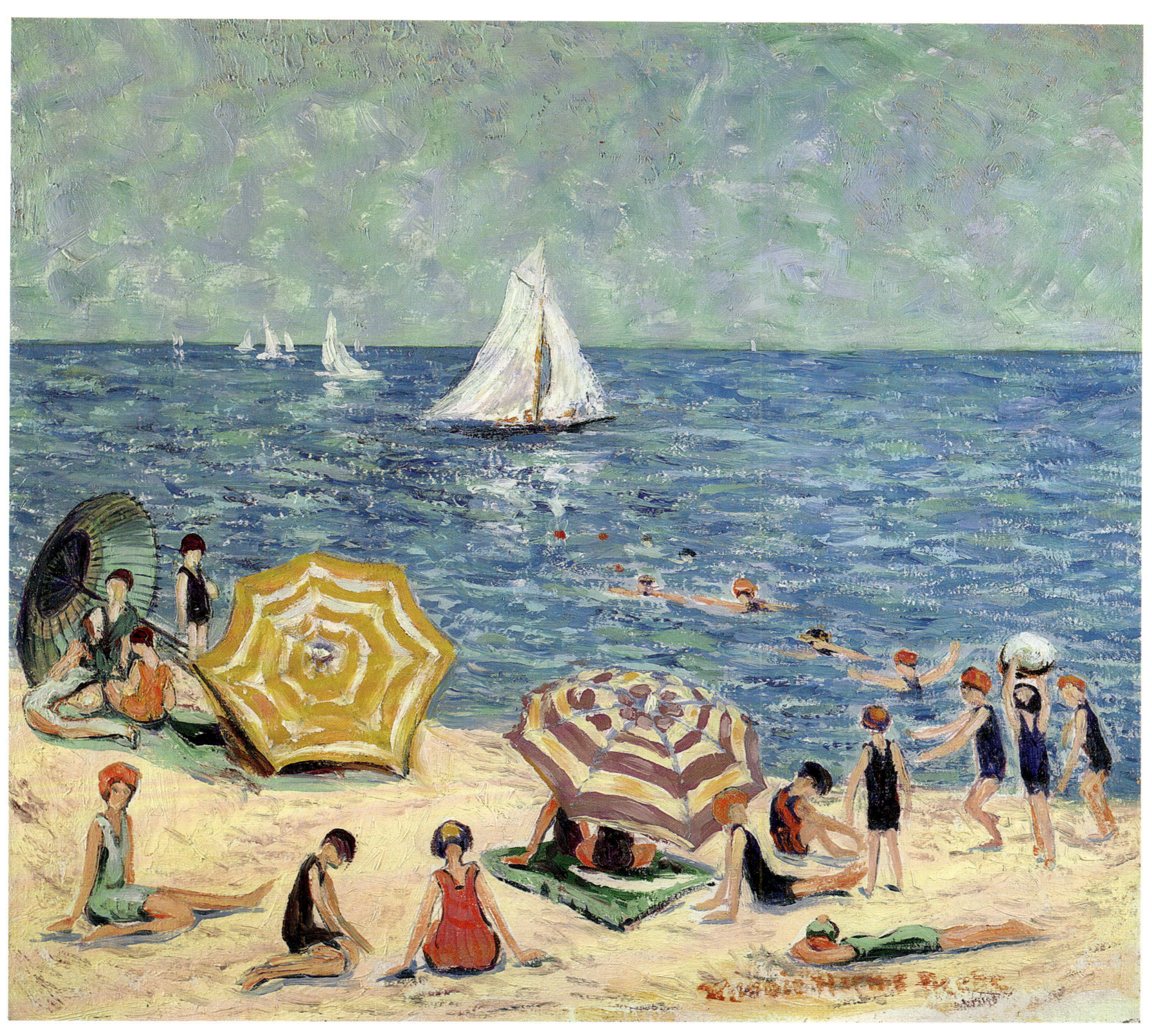

17. **Minnie Harms Neebe** (1873–1936)
Oak Street Beach, ca. 1914, oil on canvas, 22¼ × 28¾ inches

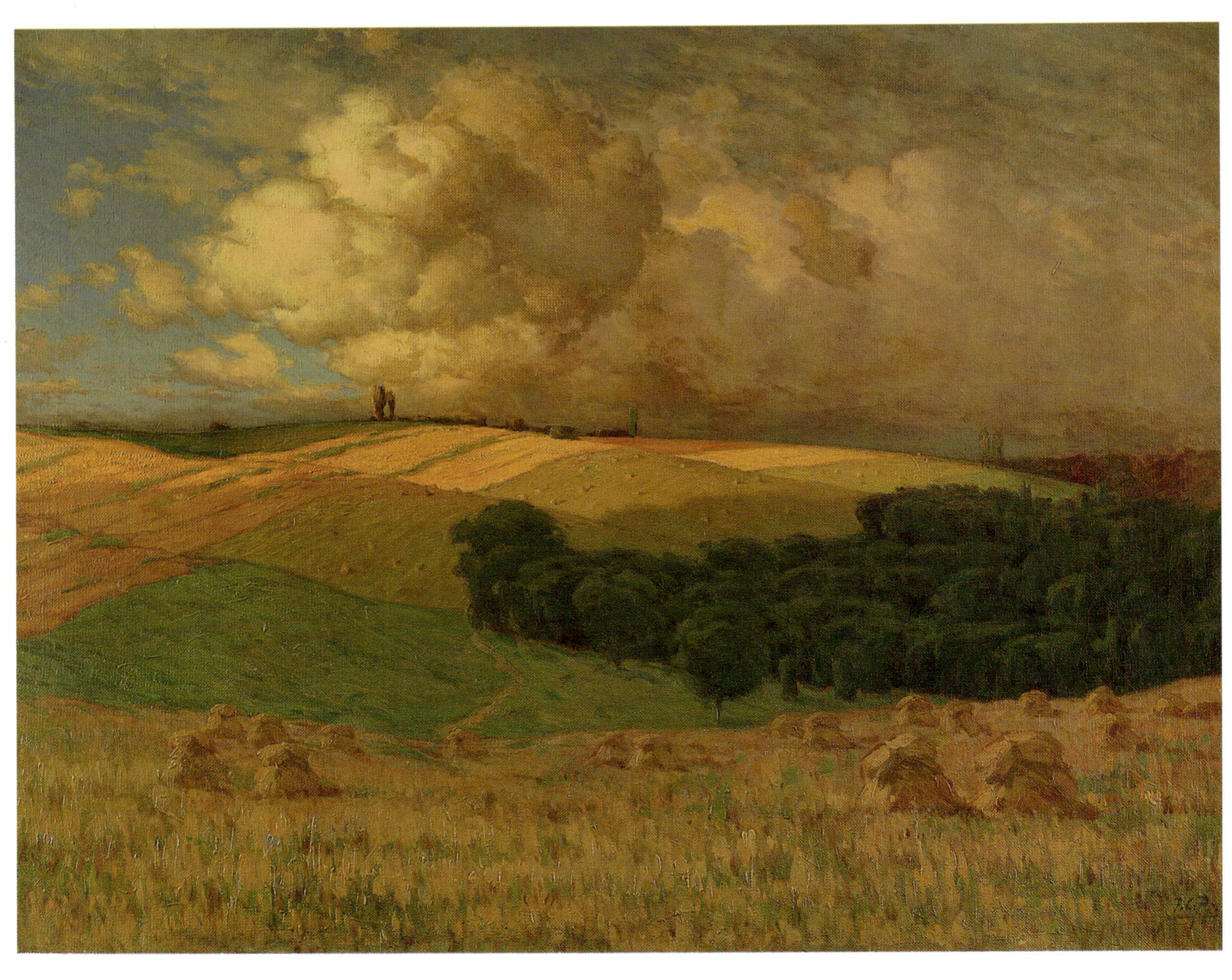

18. **Frank Charles Peyraud** (1858–1948)
October, ca. 1915, oil on canvas, 24 × 32 inches

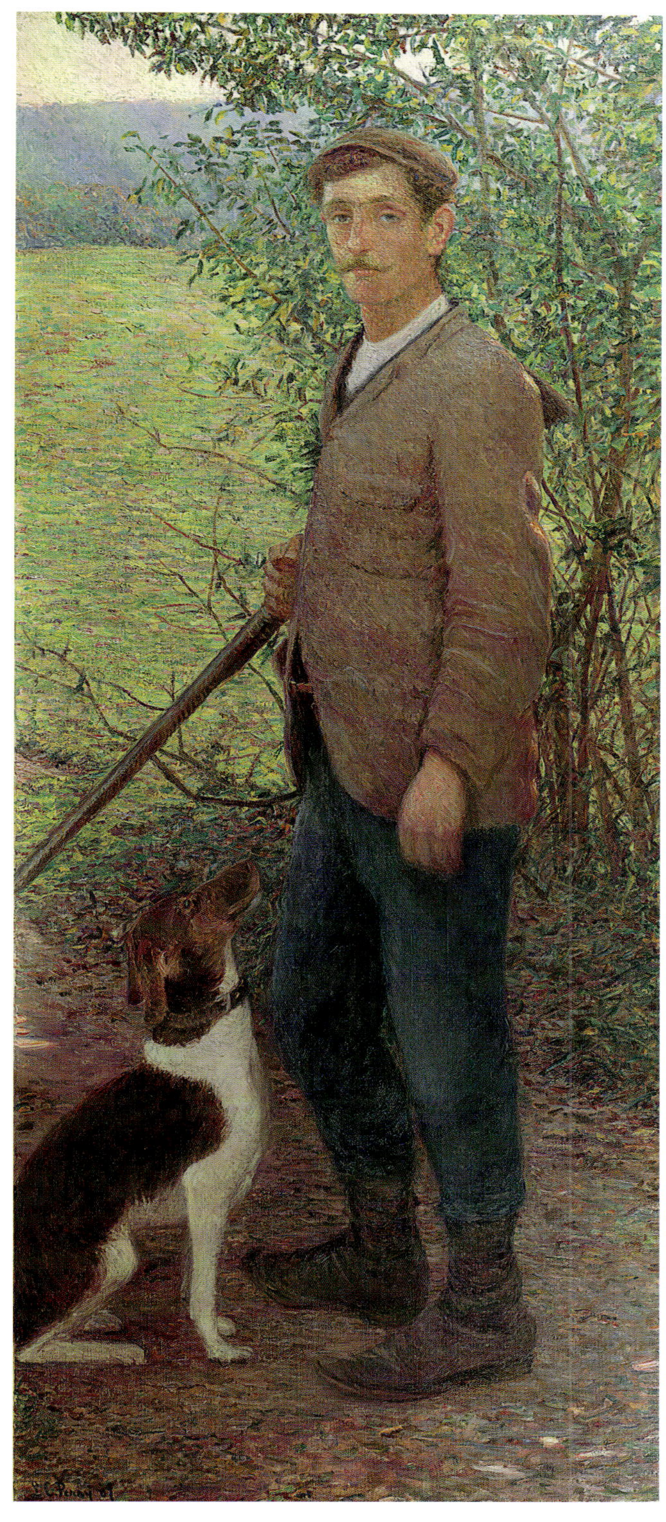

19. **Lilla Cabot Perry** (1848–1933)
The Poacher, 1907, oil on canvas, 84 × 36½ inches

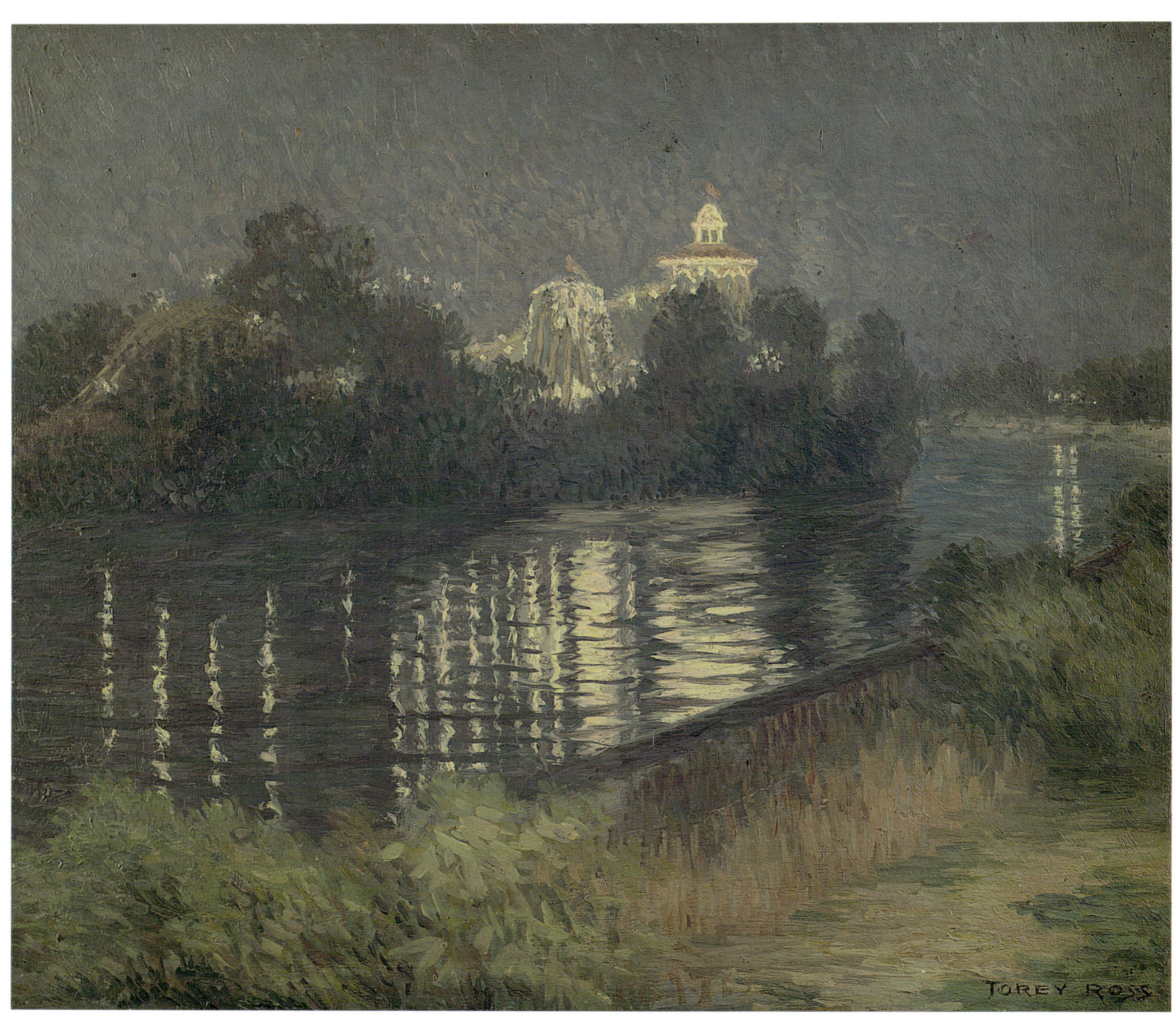

20. **Torey Ross** (1875–1966)
Riverview Park, ca. 1930, oil on panel, 14 × 16 inches

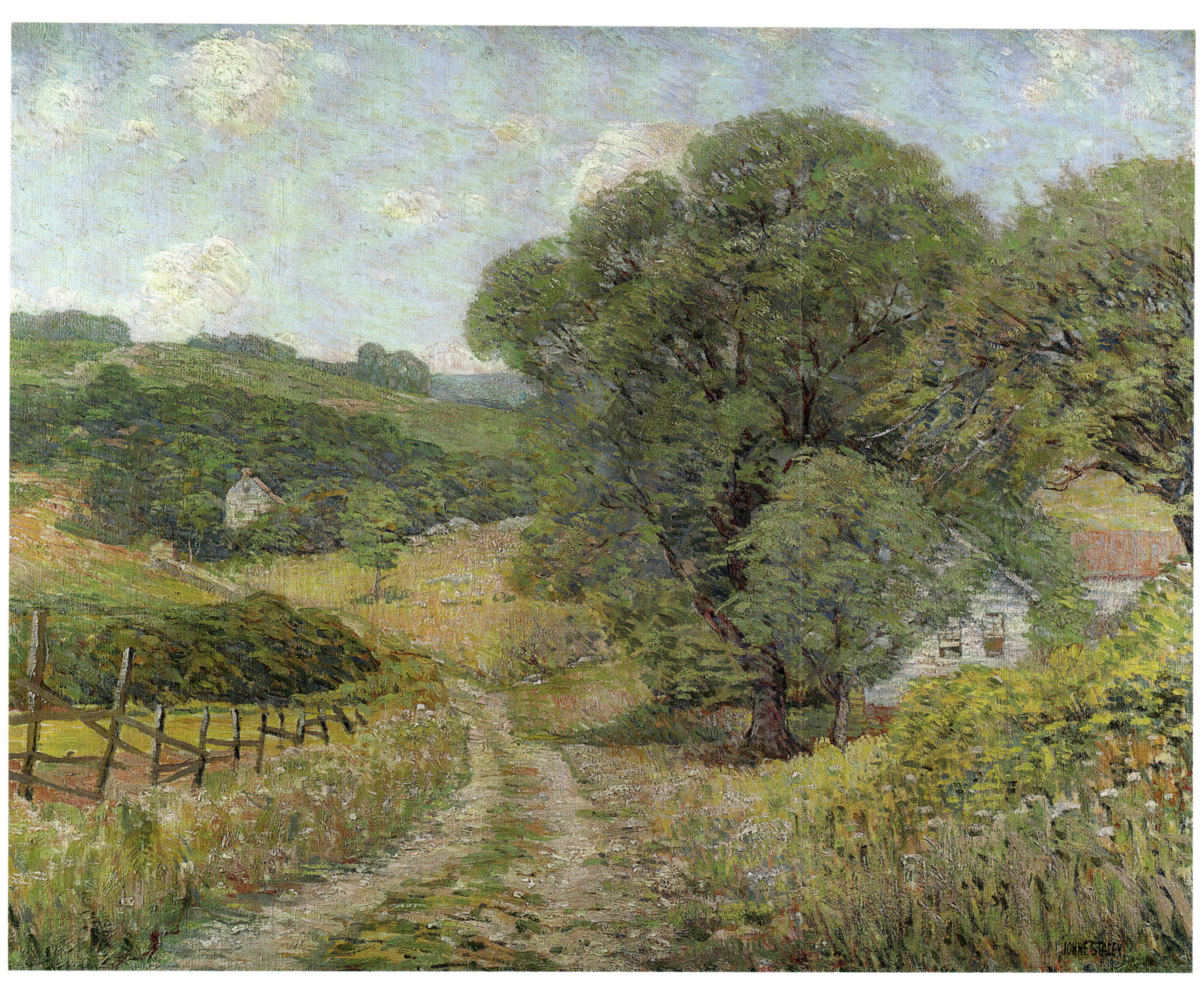

21. **John Franklin Stacey** (1859–1941)
Country Lane, ca. 1915, oil on canvas, 28 × 36 inches

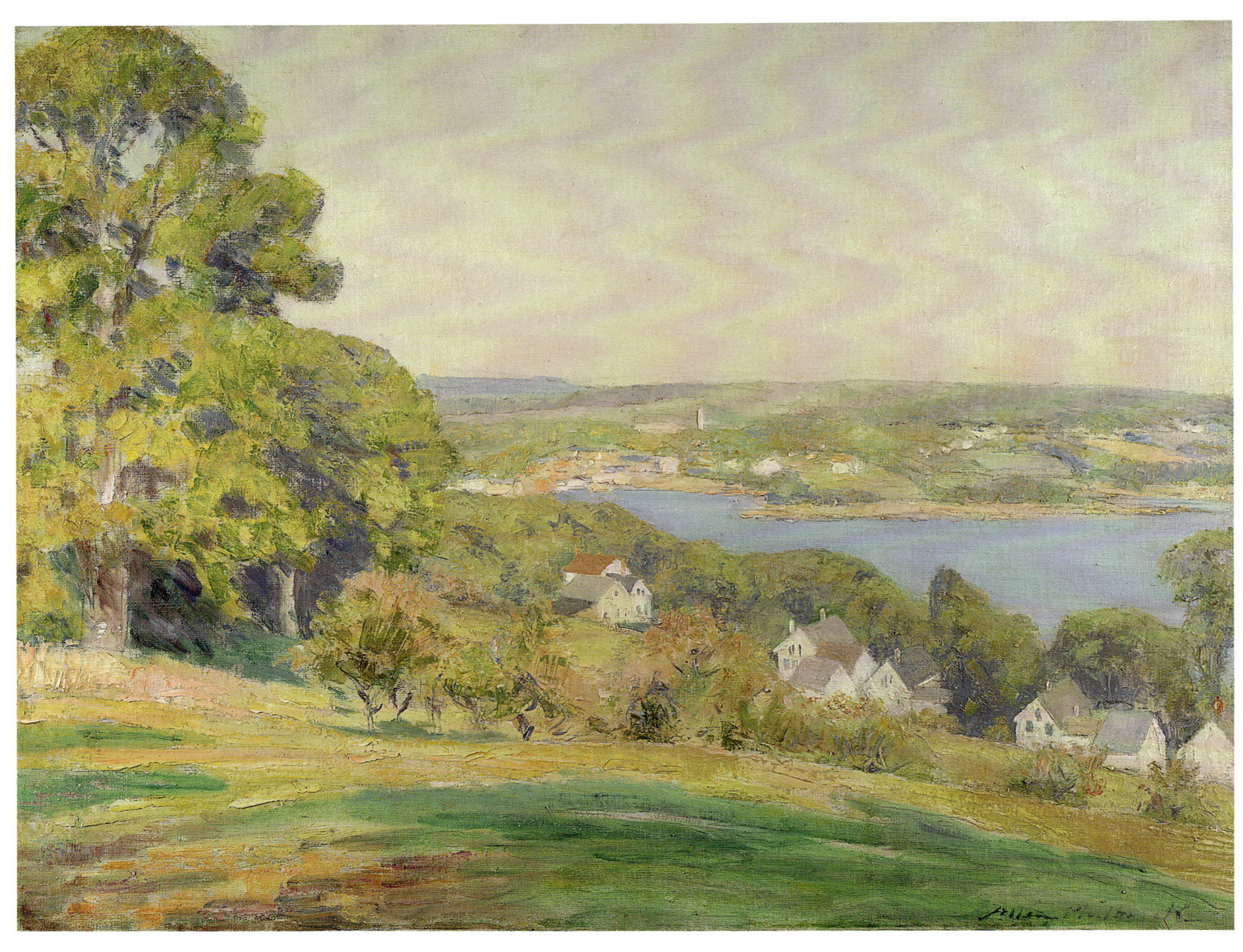

22. **Allen Philbrick** (1879–1964)
View of the Damariscotta River, Maine, ca. 1910, oil on canvas, 28 × 36 inches

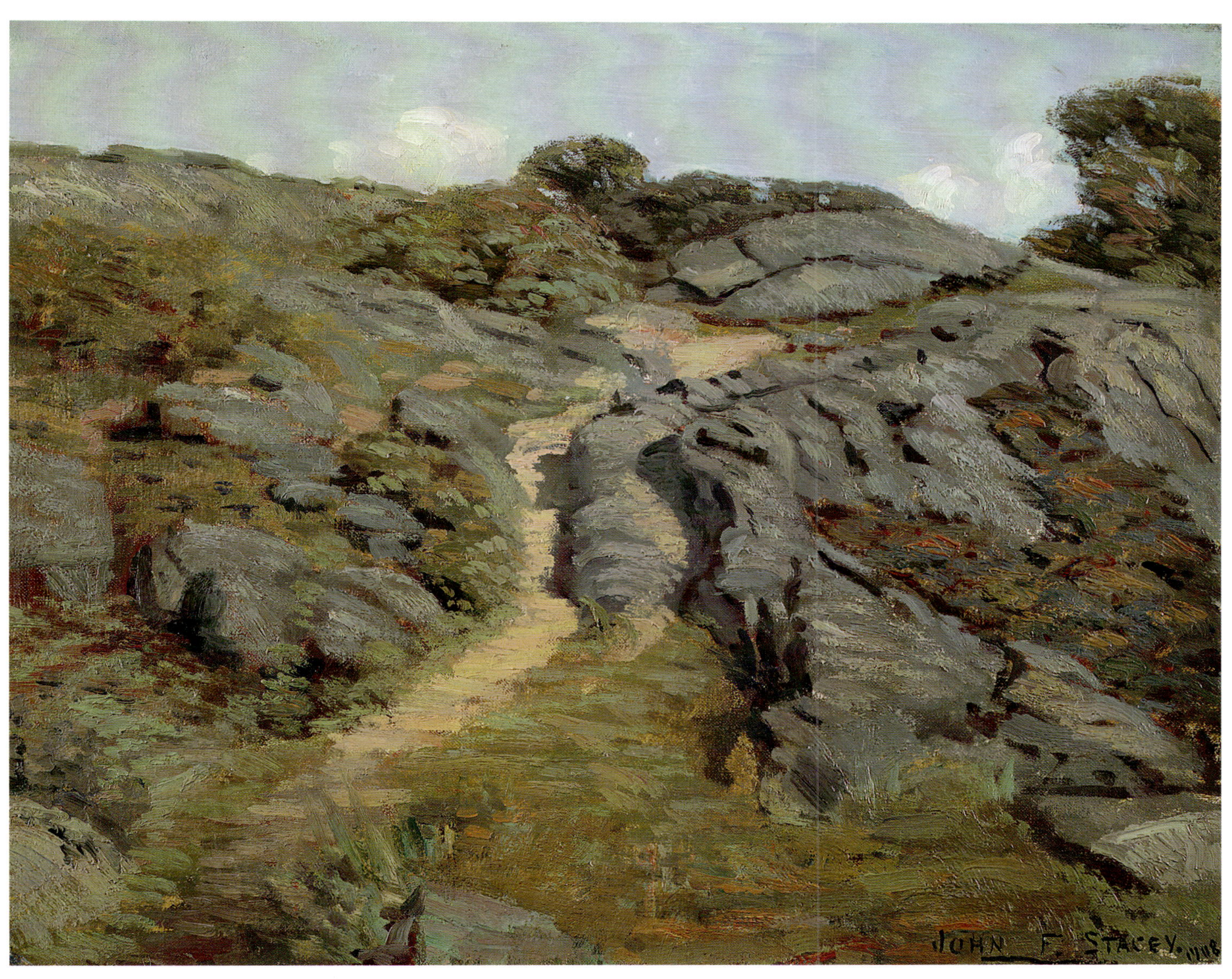

23. **John Franklin Stacey** (1859–1941)
September on the Hillside, 1908, oil on canvas, 16 × 20 inches

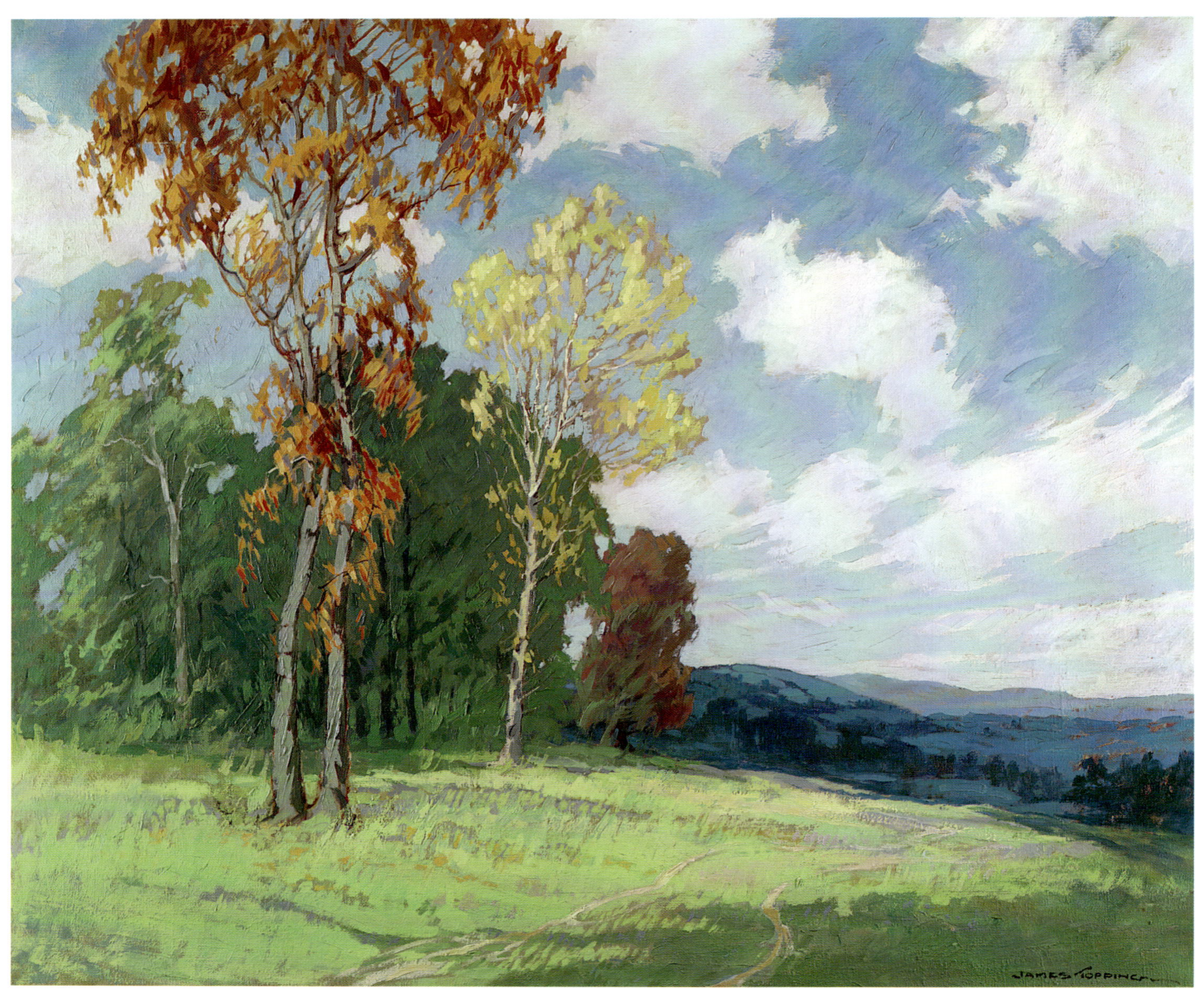

24. **James Topping** (1879–1948)
A Touch of Autumn, ca. 1925, oil on canvas, 30 × 36 inches

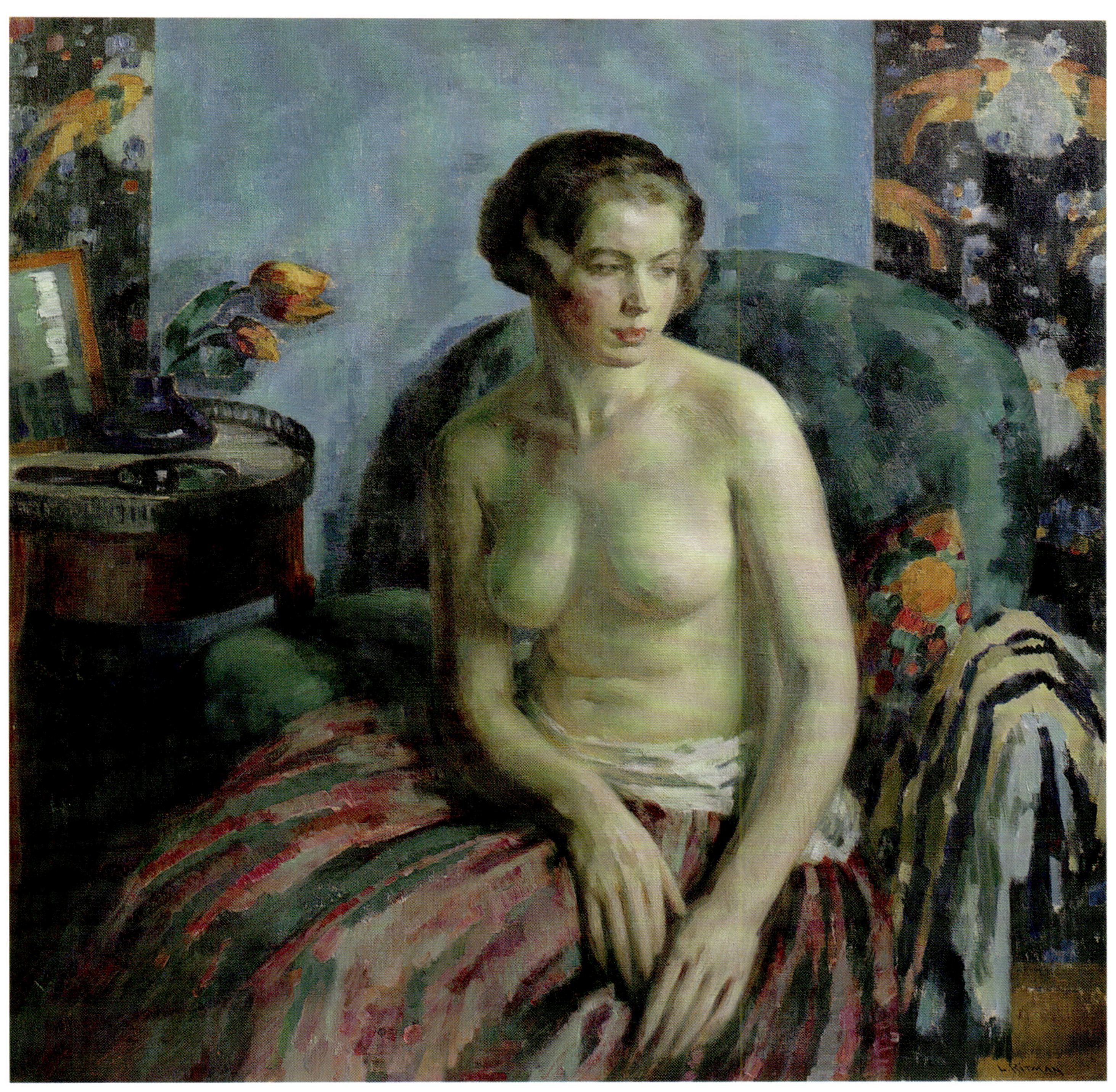

25. **Louis Ritman** (1889–1963)
René, ca. 1925, oil on canvas, 39½ × 39½ inches

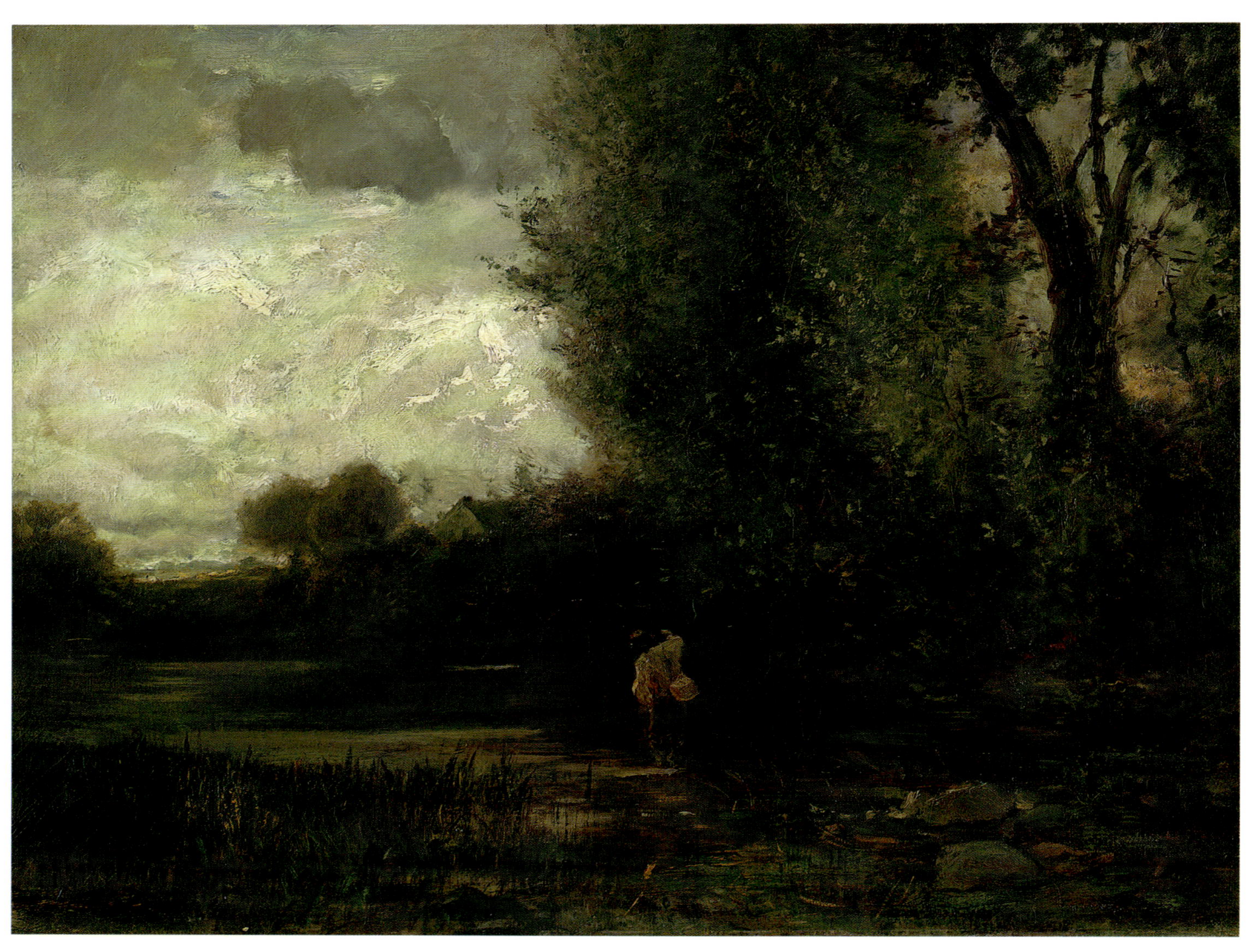

26. **Arthur Parton** (1842–1914)
Angler by Forest Stream, ca. 1870s, oil on canvas, 18½ × 20¼ inches

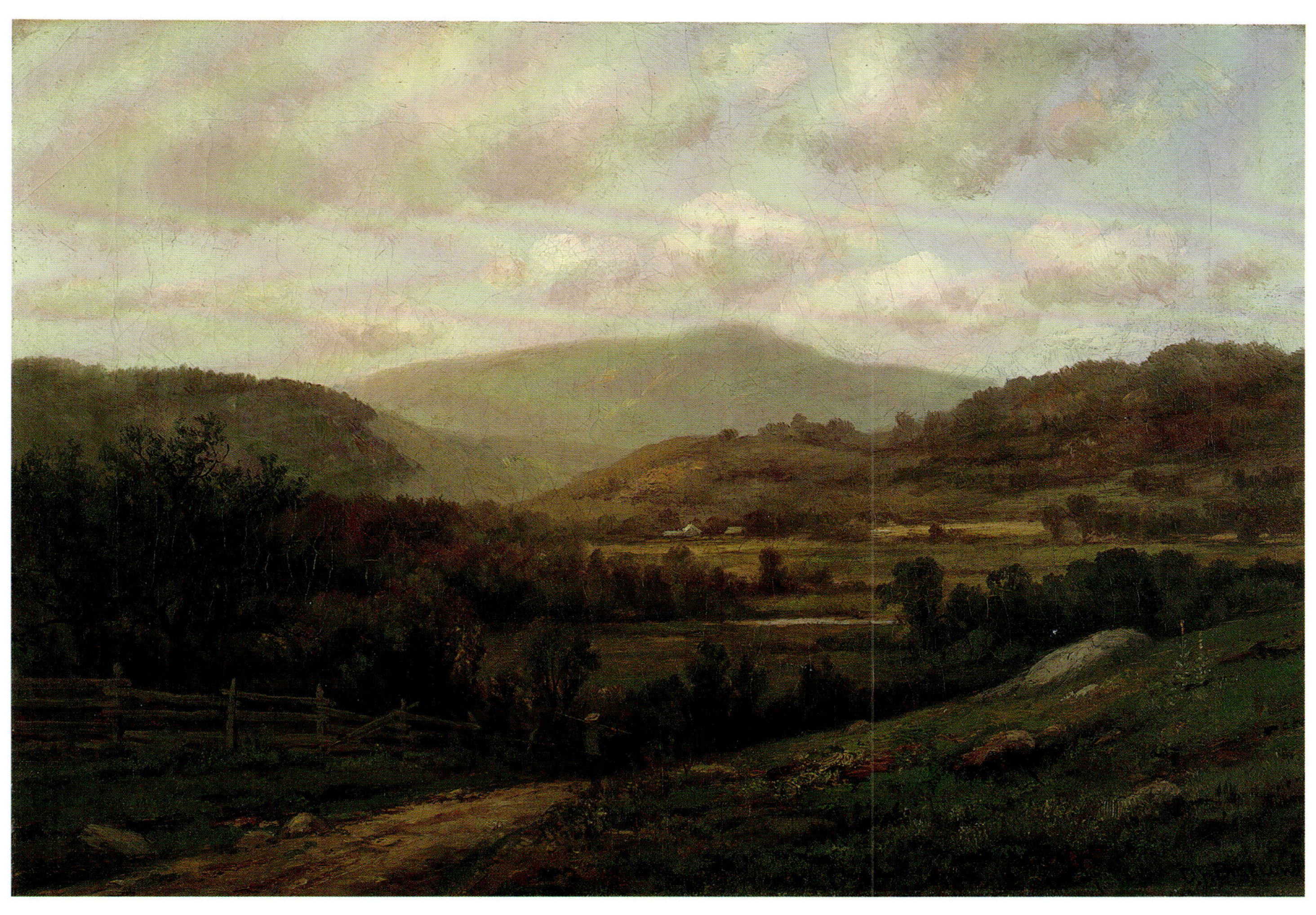

27. **Daniel Folger Bigelow** (1823–1910)
New England Landscape, ca. 1880, oil on canvas, 14 × 20 inches

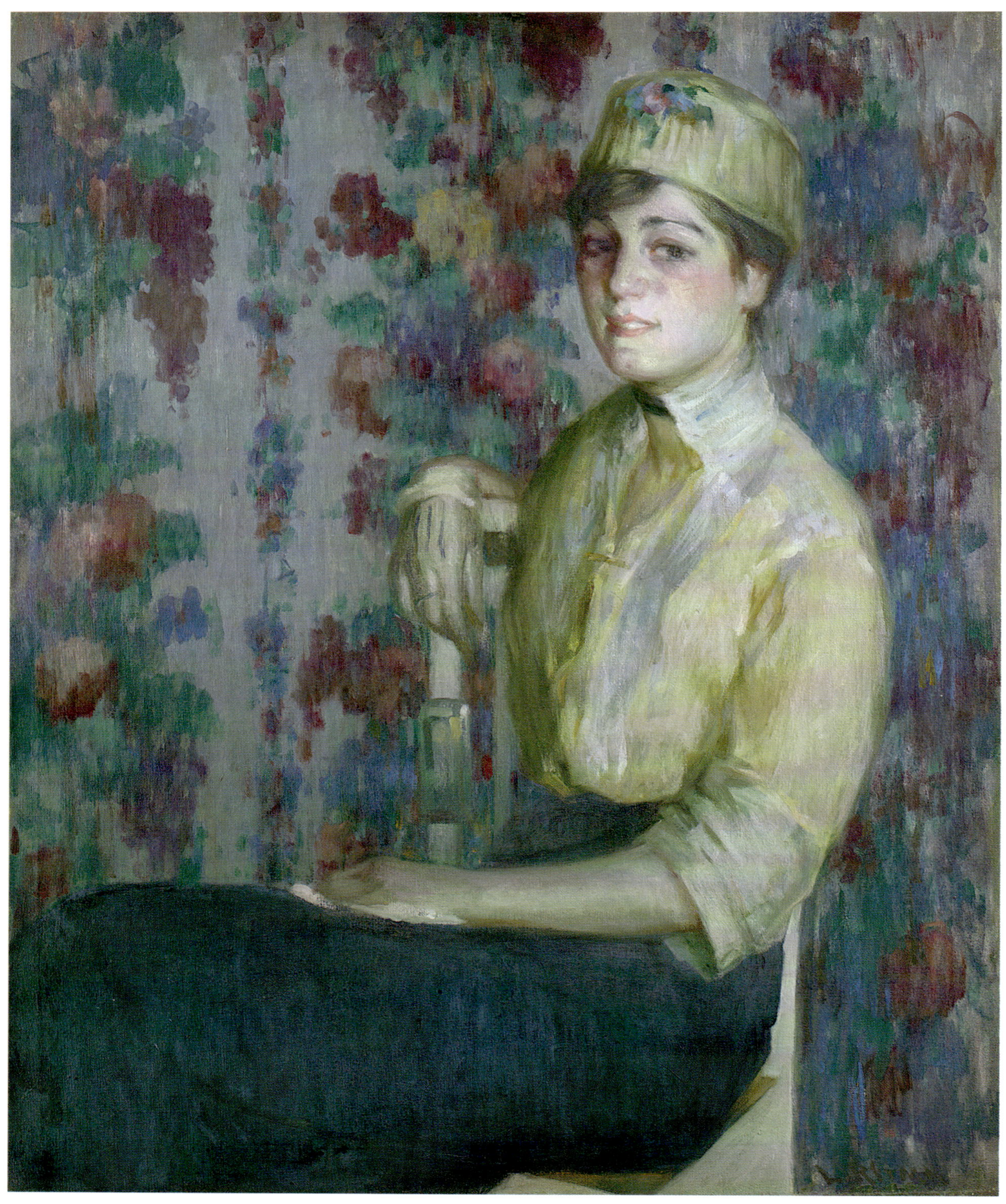

28. **Louis Ritman** (1889–1963)
Jean, ca. 1920s, oil on canvas, 29 × 35½ inches

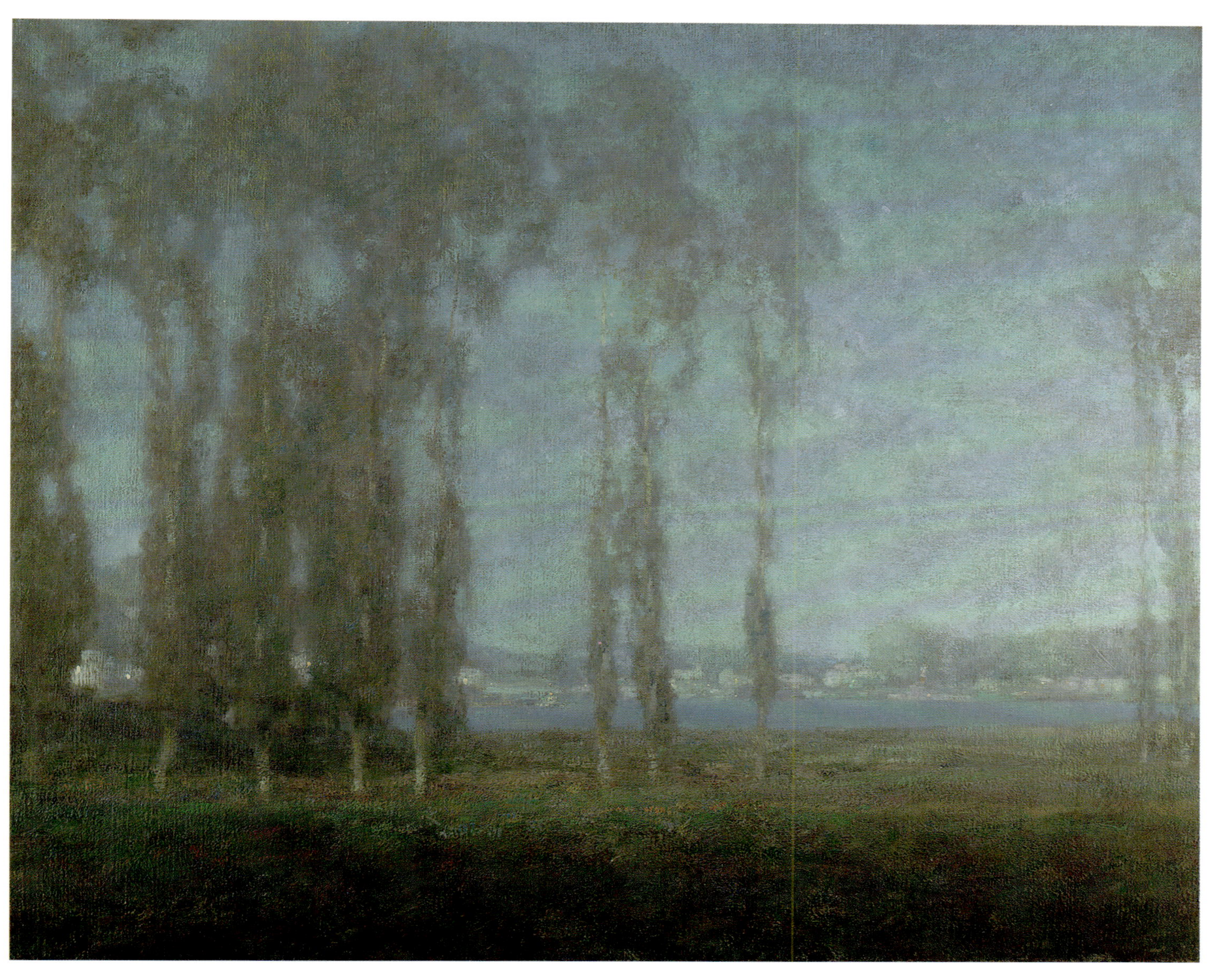

29. **Lawrence Mazzanovich** (1872–1959)
Moonlight at Dawn, ca. 1908, oil on canvas, 32 × 39½ inches

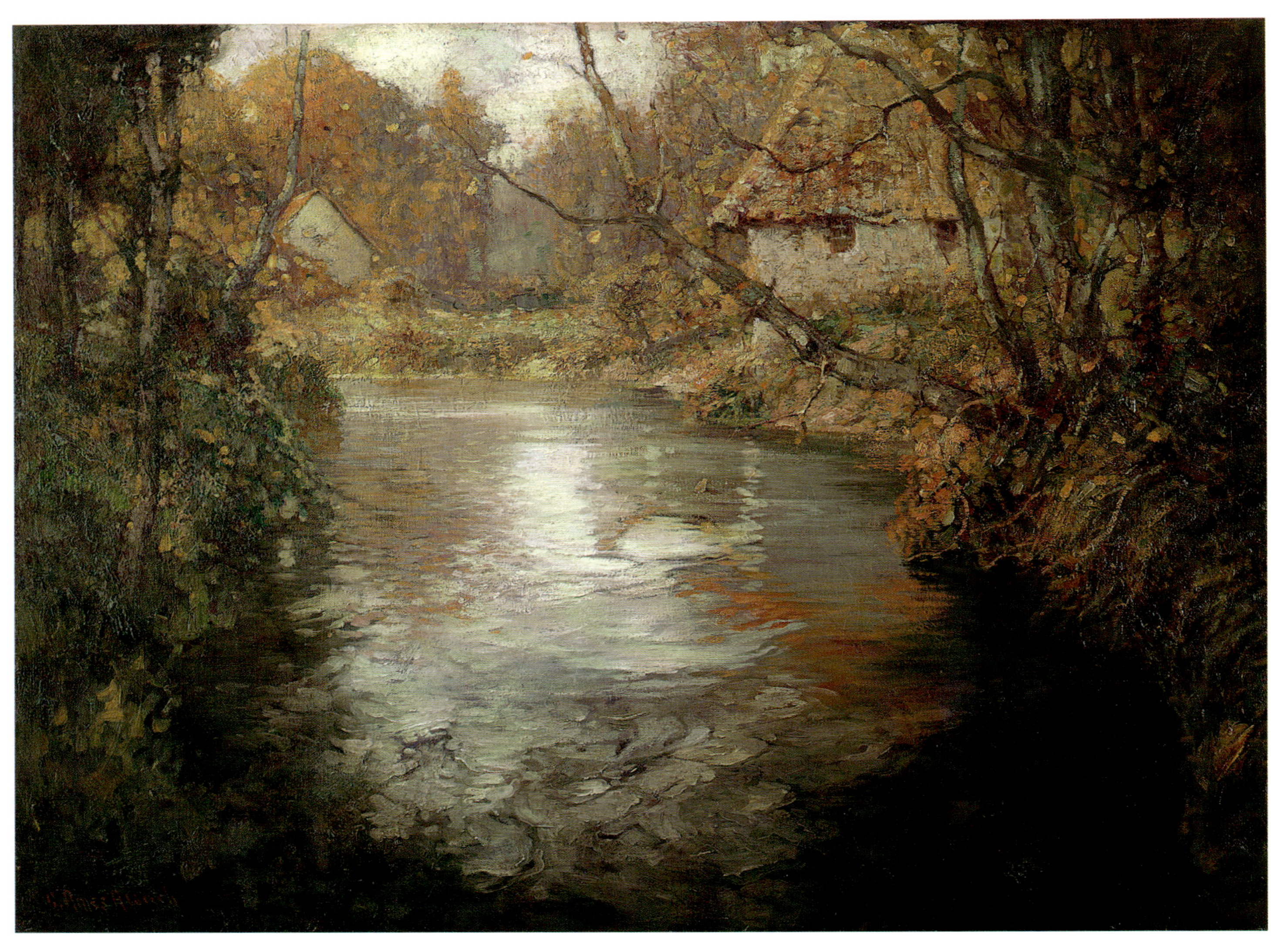

30. **George Ames Aldrich** (1872–1941)
Normandy River Landscape, ca. 1905, oil on canvas, 30 × 40 inches

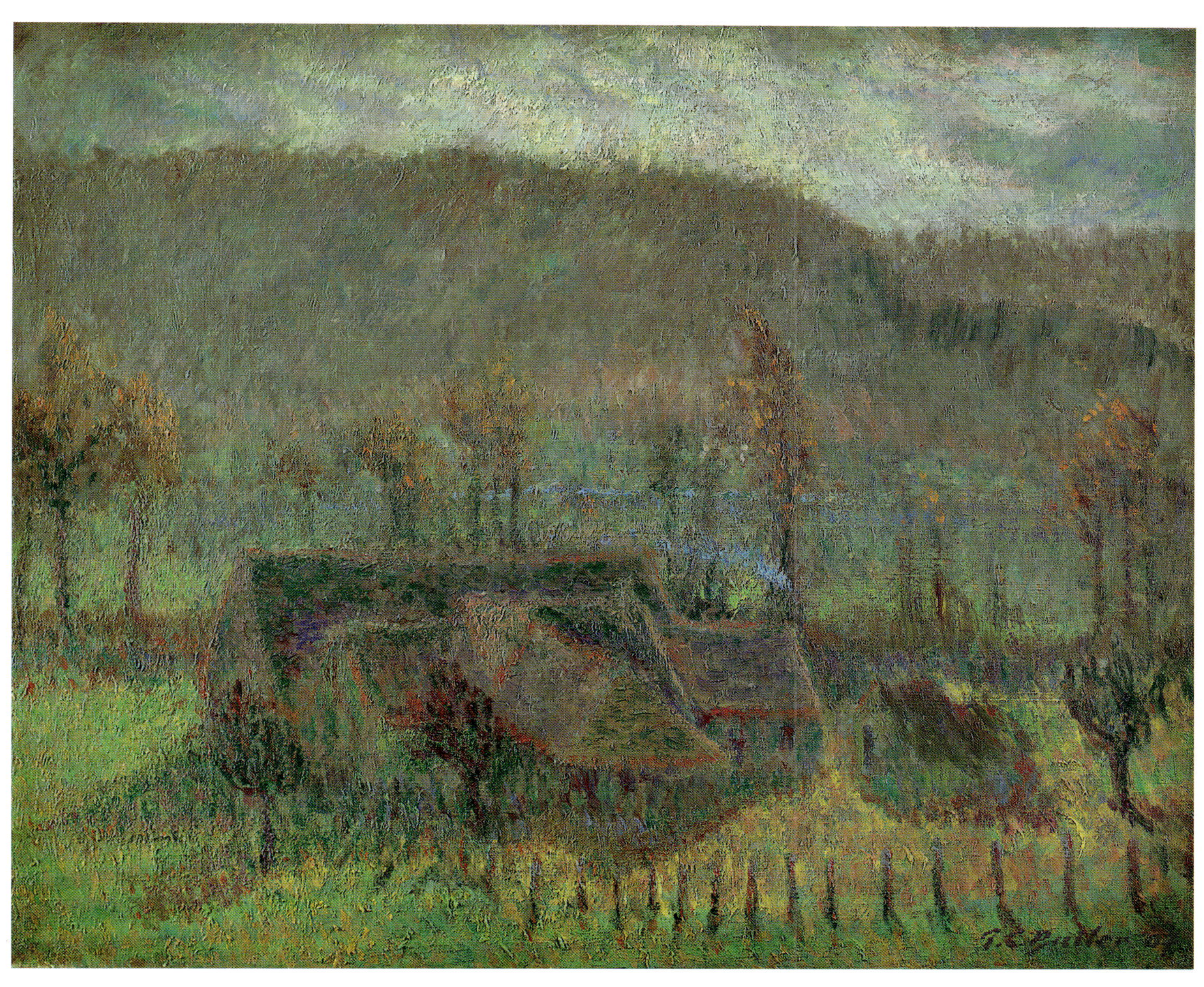

31. **Theodore Earl Butler** (1861–1936)
Valley Farm (Cottage in Giverny), 1907, oil on canvas, 23¾ × 29 inches

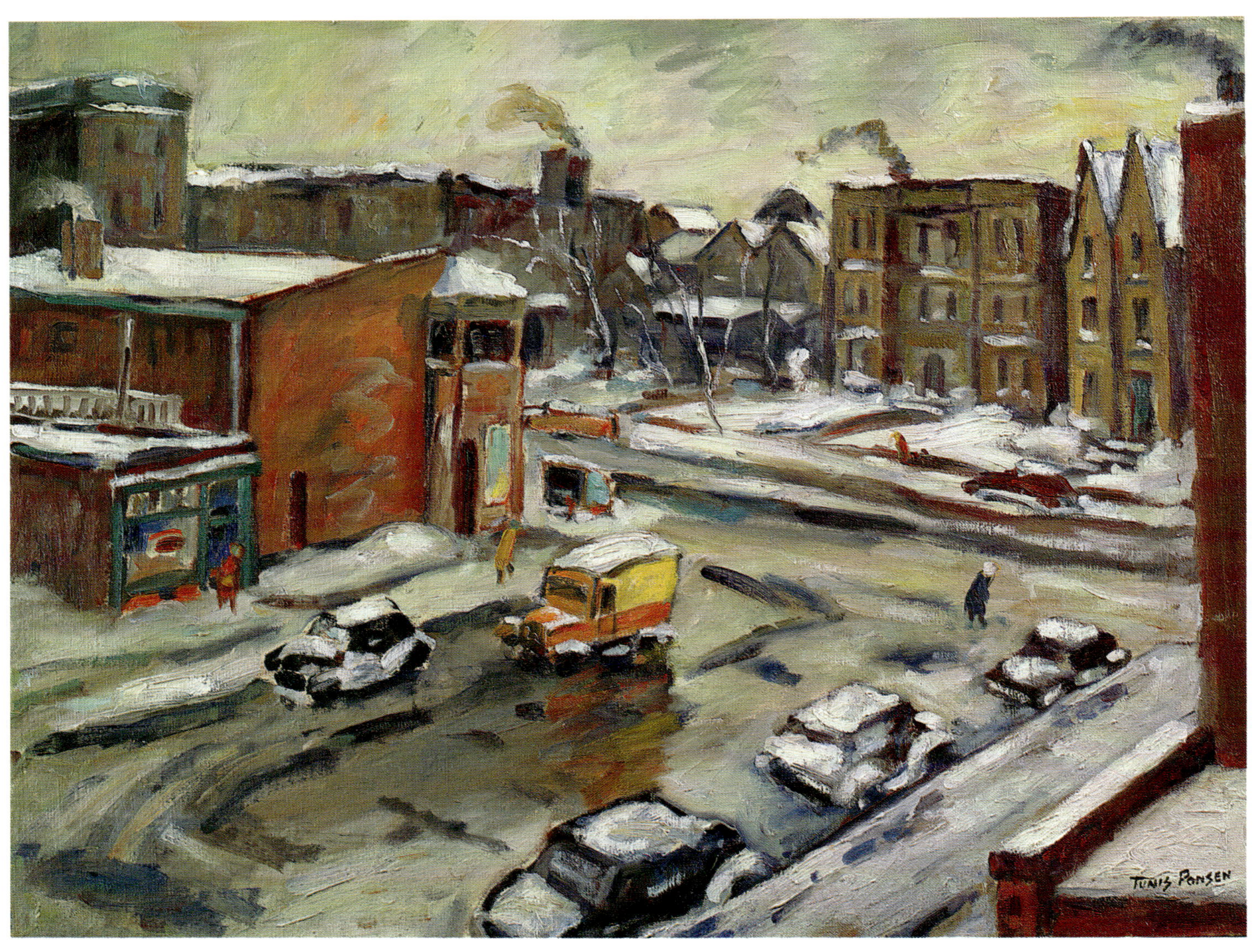

32. **Tunis Ponsen** (1891–1968)
Winter Streets, Chicago, ca. 1935, oil on canvas, 20 × 24 inches

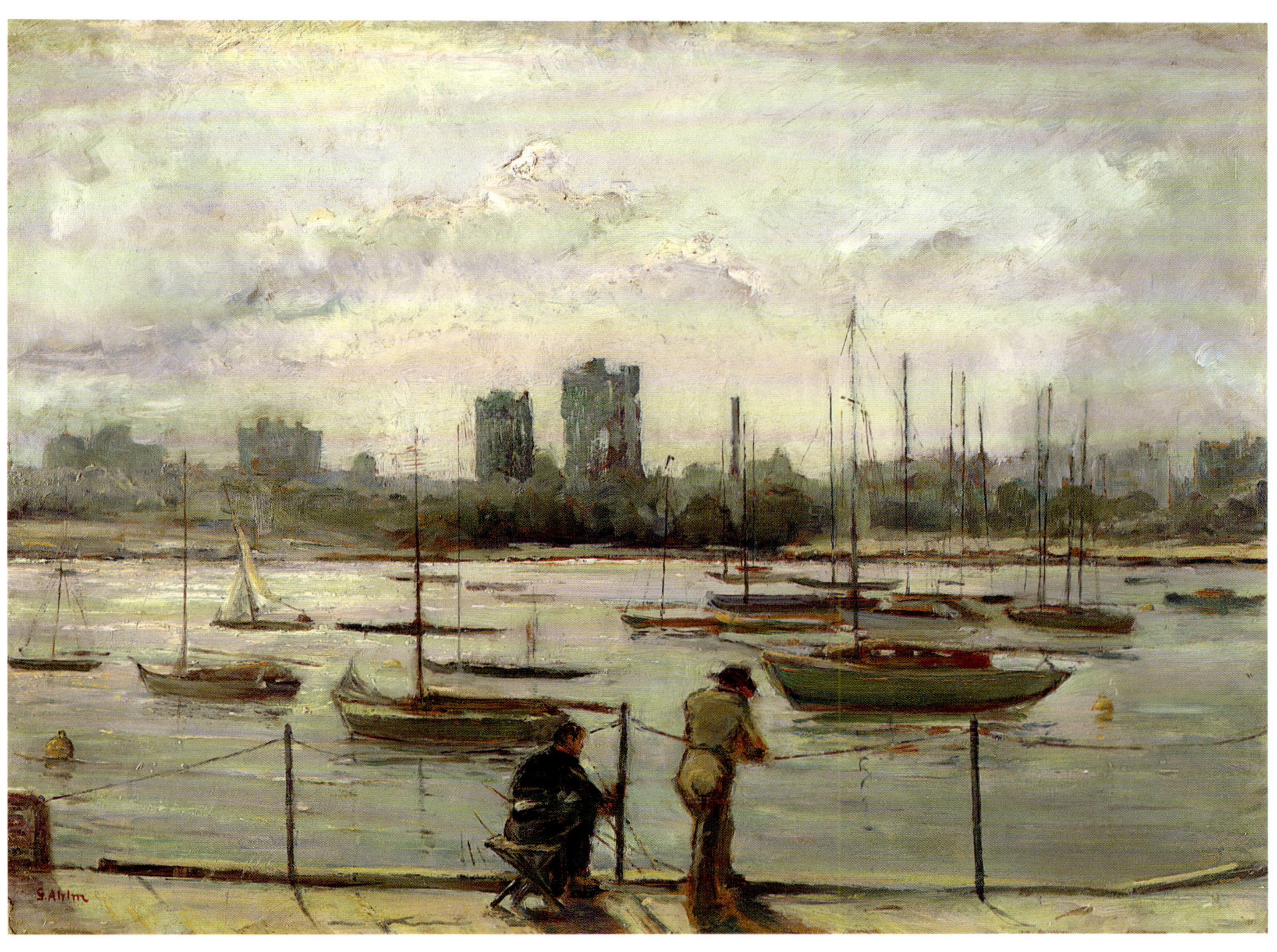

33. **Gerda-Maria Ahlm** (1869–1956)
Fishing in Chicago, ca. 1915, oil on board, 18 × 24½ inches

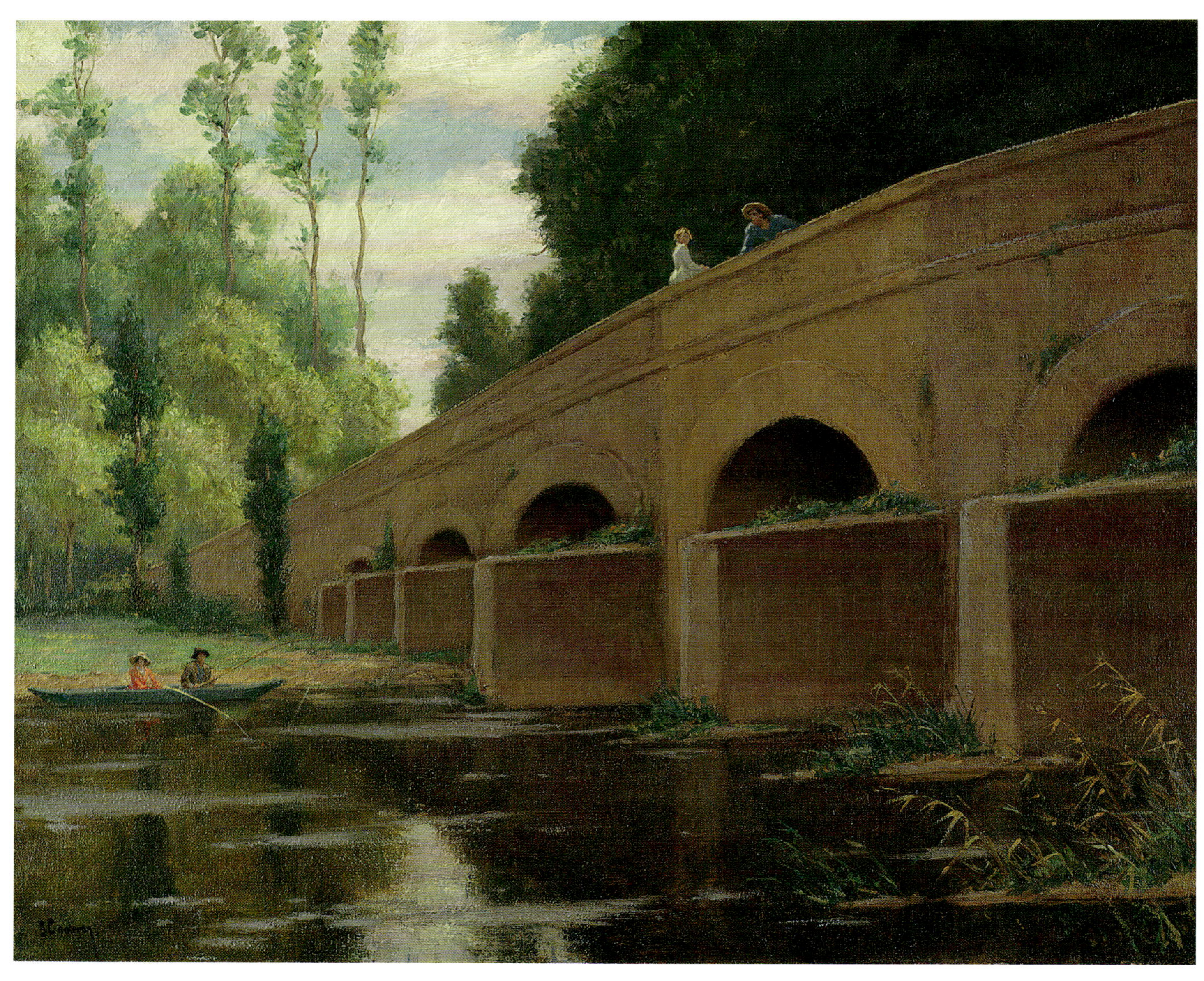

34. **Edgar S. Cameron** (1862–1944)
Bridge in the Countryside, ca. 1897, oil on canvas, 23¾ × 29 inches

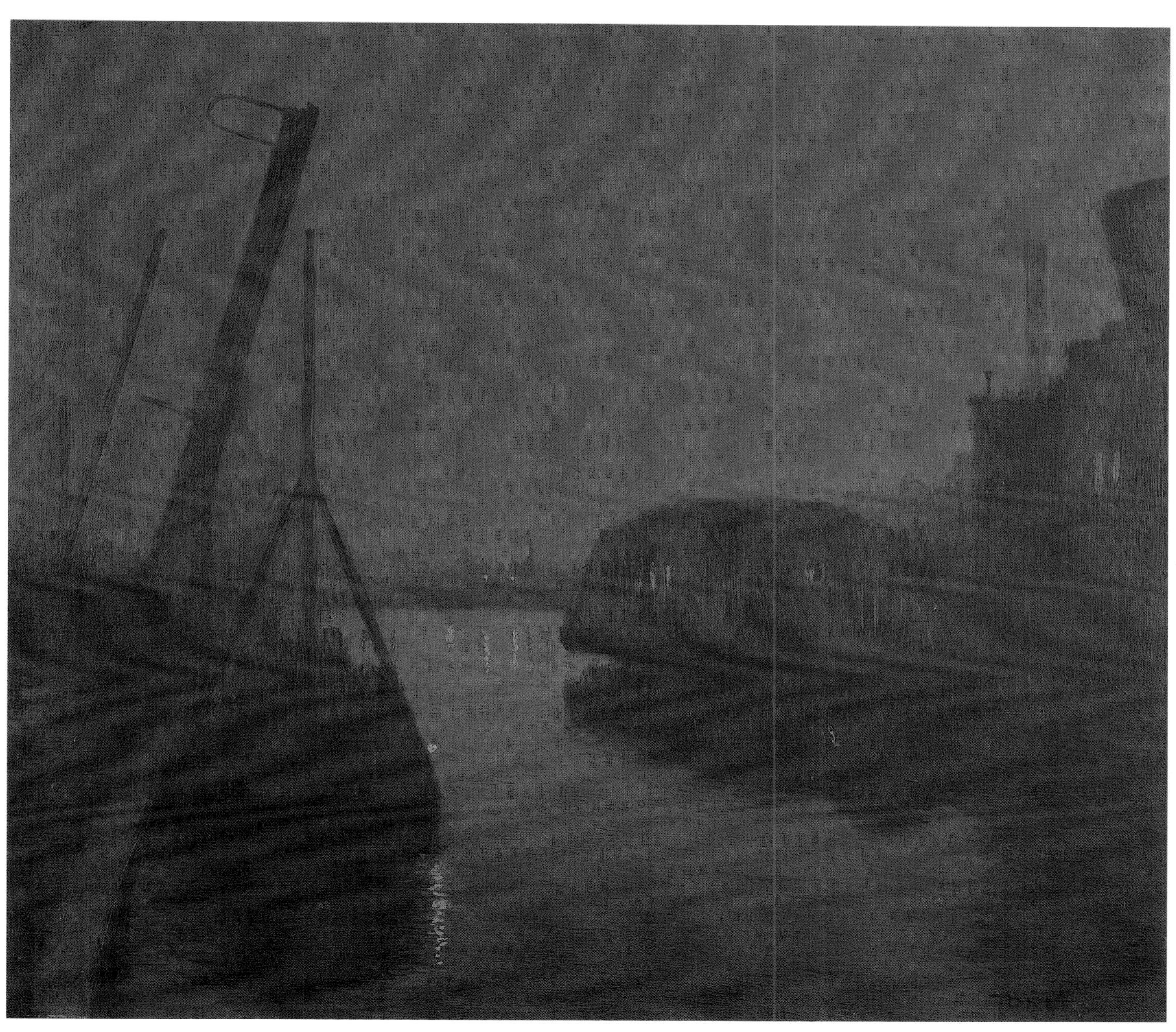

35. Torey Ross (1875–1966)
Chicago River at Night, ca. 1925, oil on panel, 14 × 16 inches

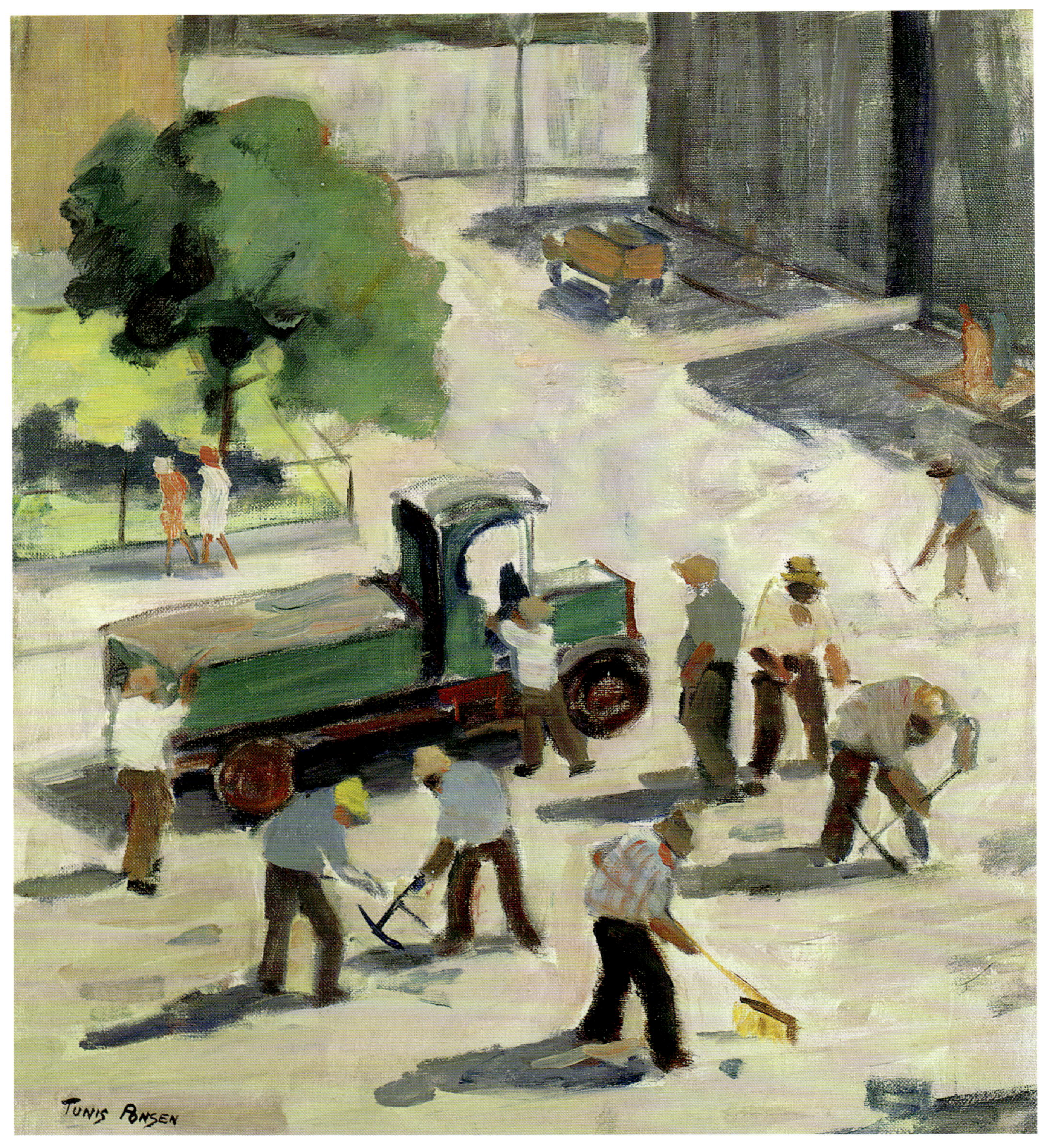

36. **Tunis Ponsen** (1891–1968)
Repair Gang, ca. 1930, oil on canvas, 18 × 16 inches

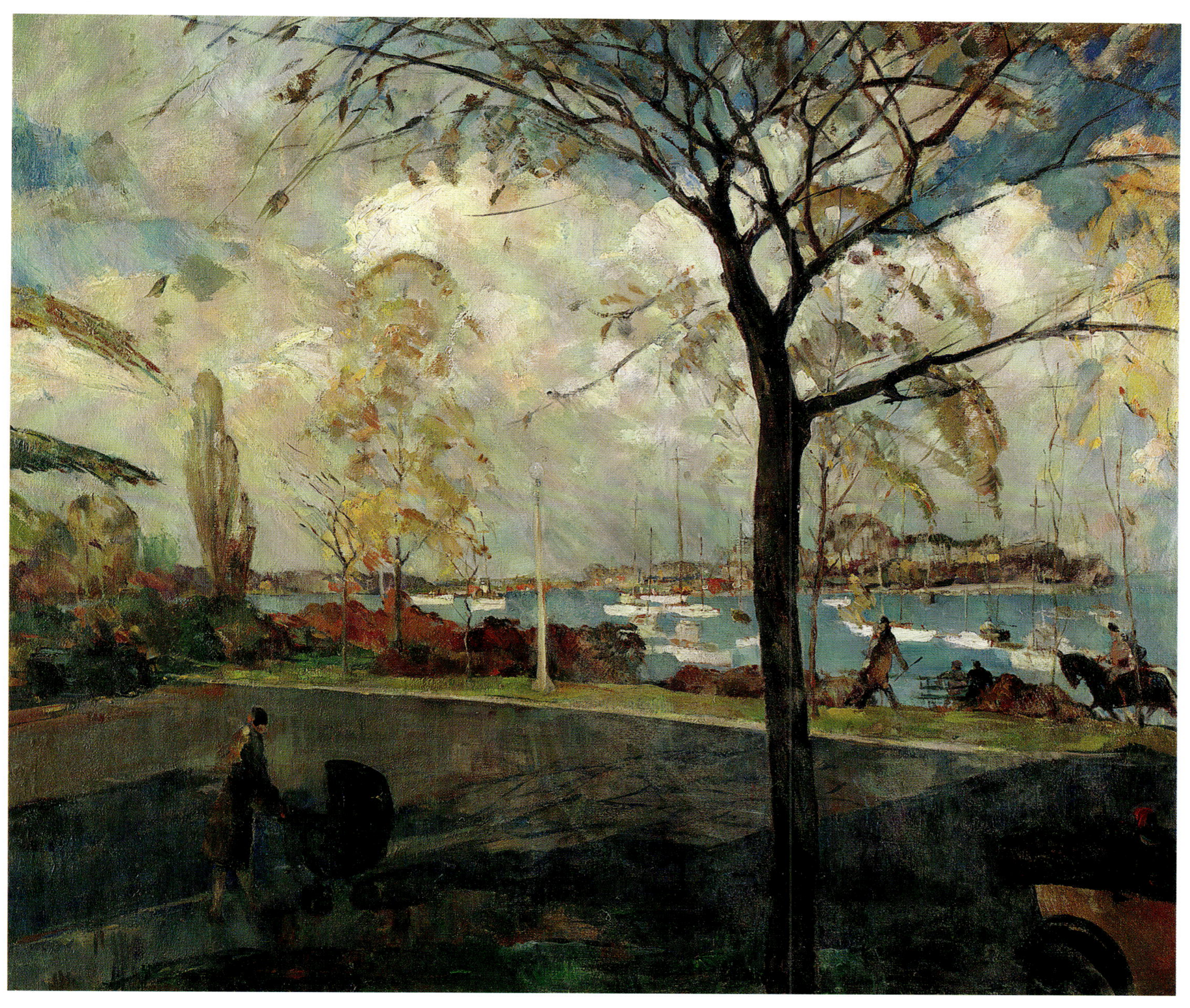

37. Francis Chapin (1899–1965)
Belmont Harbor No. 2, ca. 1928, oil on canvas, 30¼ × 35 inches

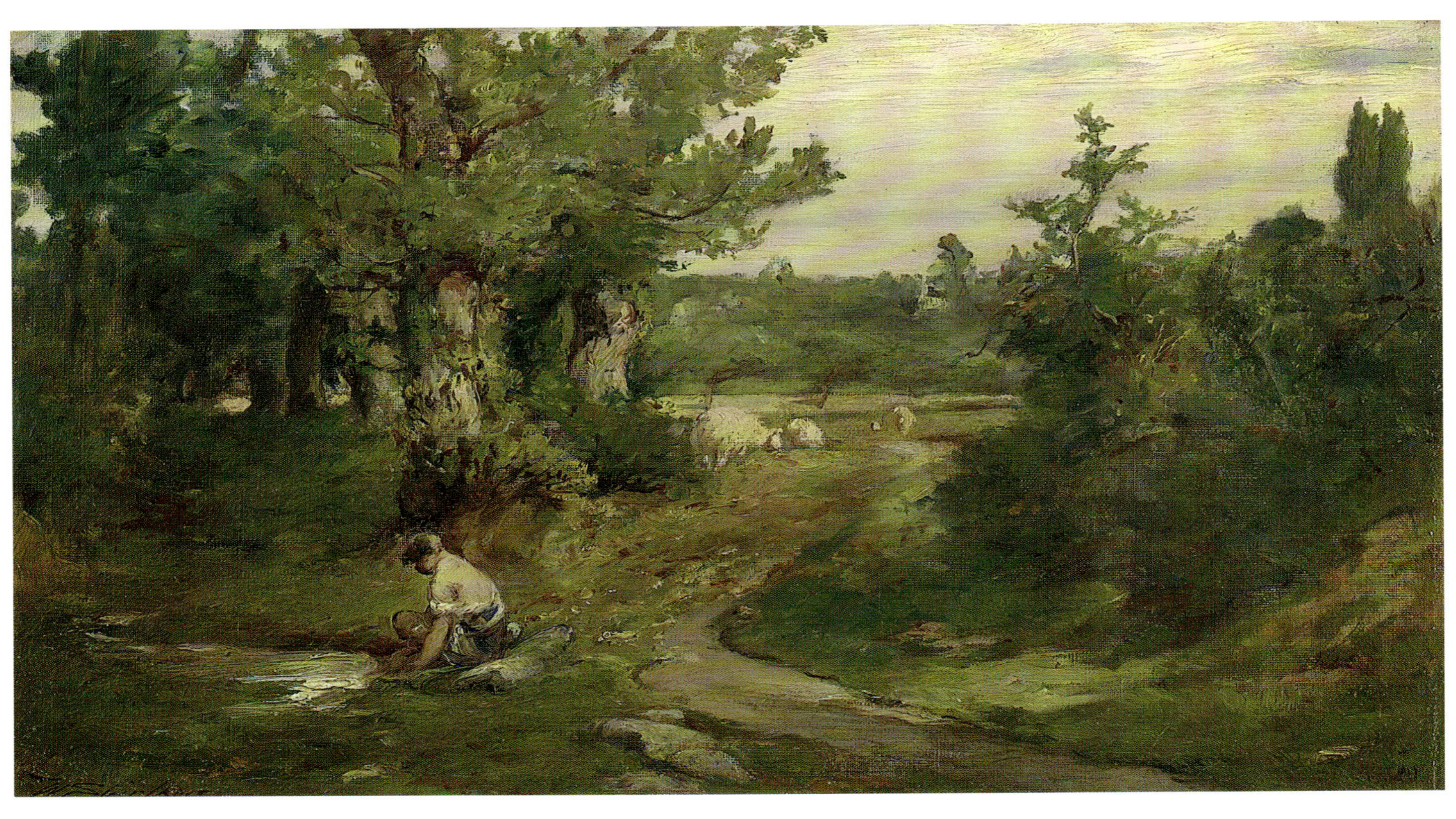

38. **Walter Shirlaw** (1838–1909)
Little Shepherd, ca. 1885, oil on canvas, 10⅞ × 19½ inches

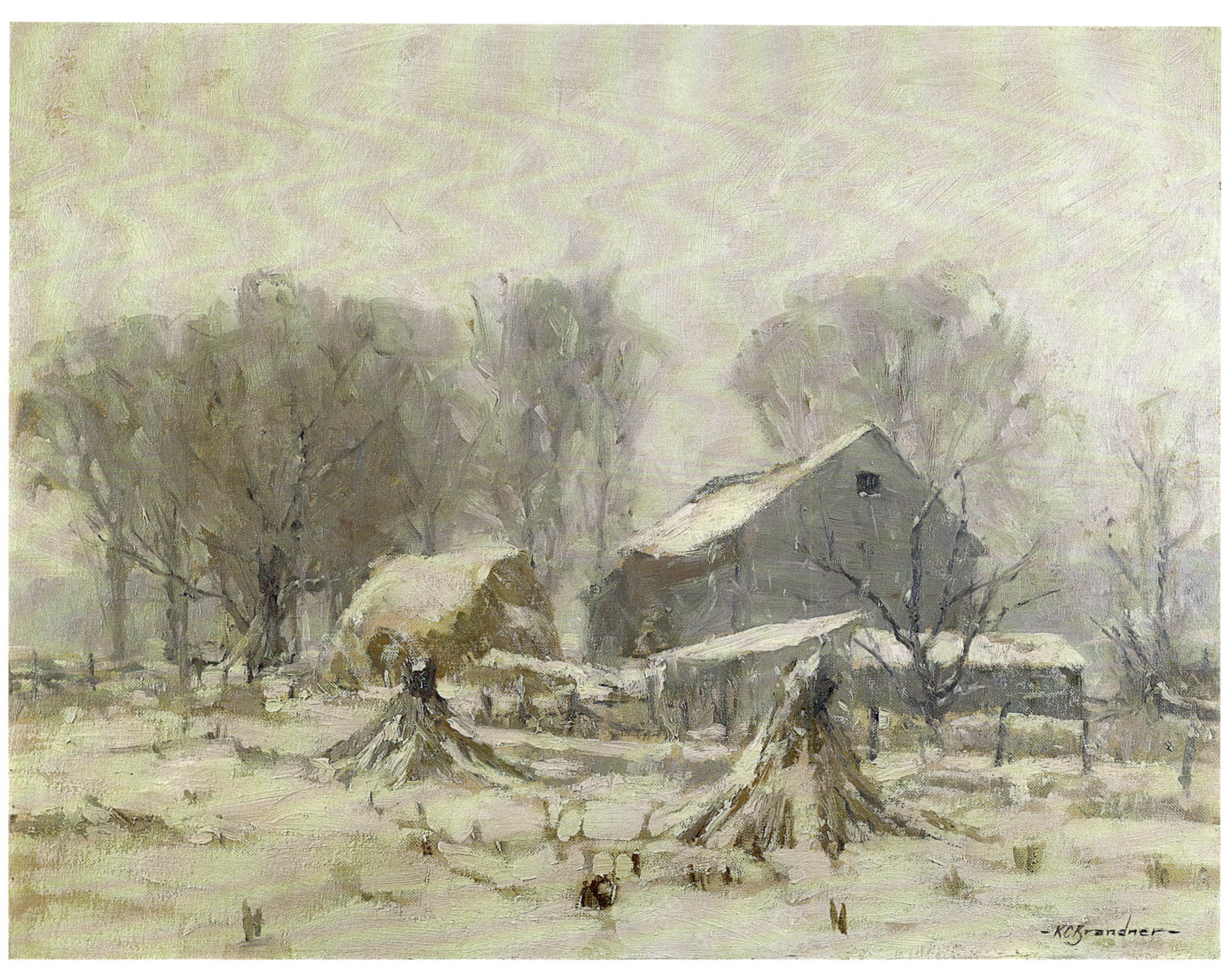

39. Karl C. F. Brandner (1898–1961)
Farmhouse in the Snow, ca. 1945, oil on canvas, 16 × 20 inches

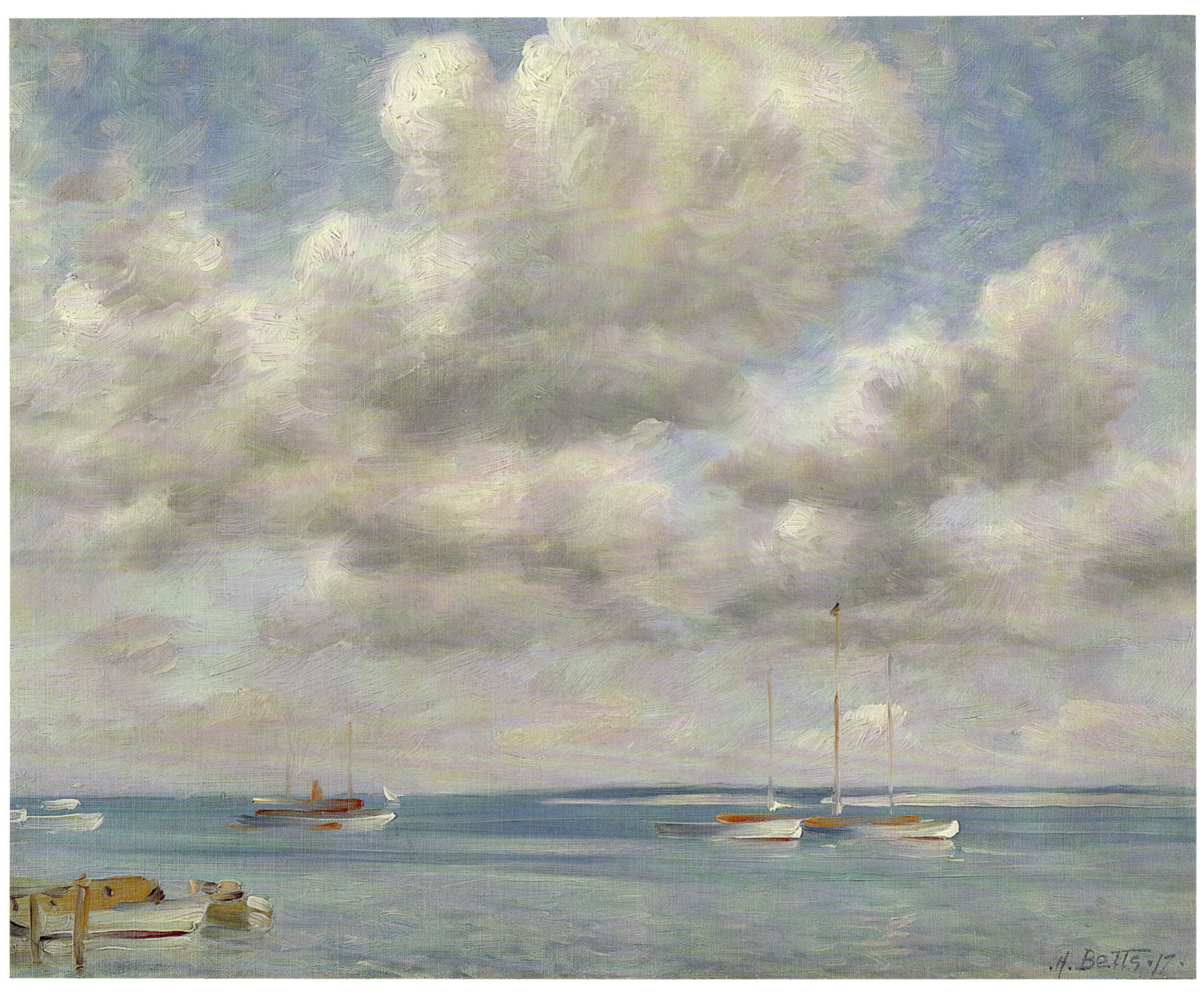

40. **Harold Betts** (1883–1963)
Clouds Forming over Lake Michigan, 1917, oil on canvas, 20 × 24 inches

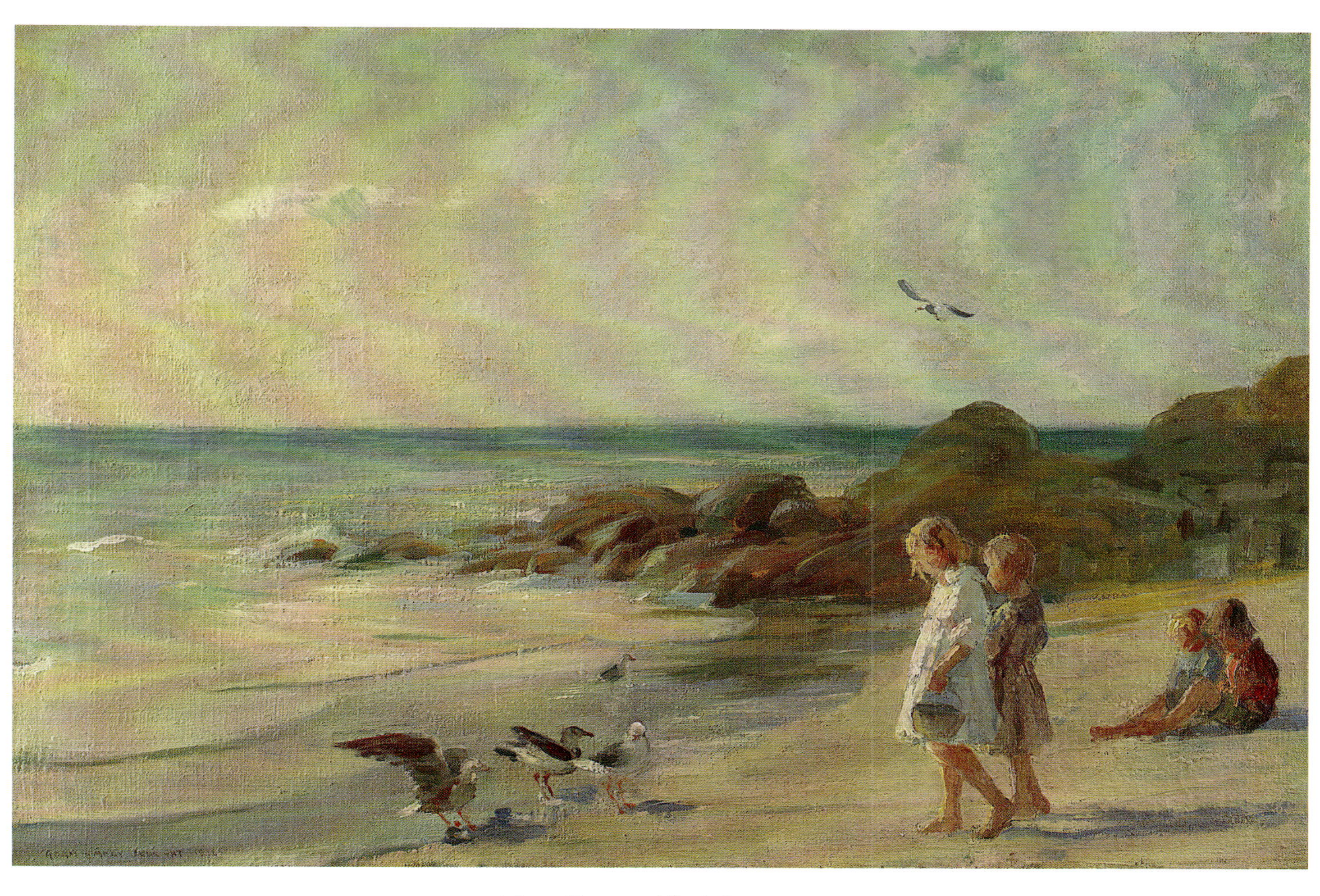

41. **Adam Emory Albright** (1862–1957)
Children Playing on a Sandy Shore, 1922, oil on canvas, 20 × 30 inches

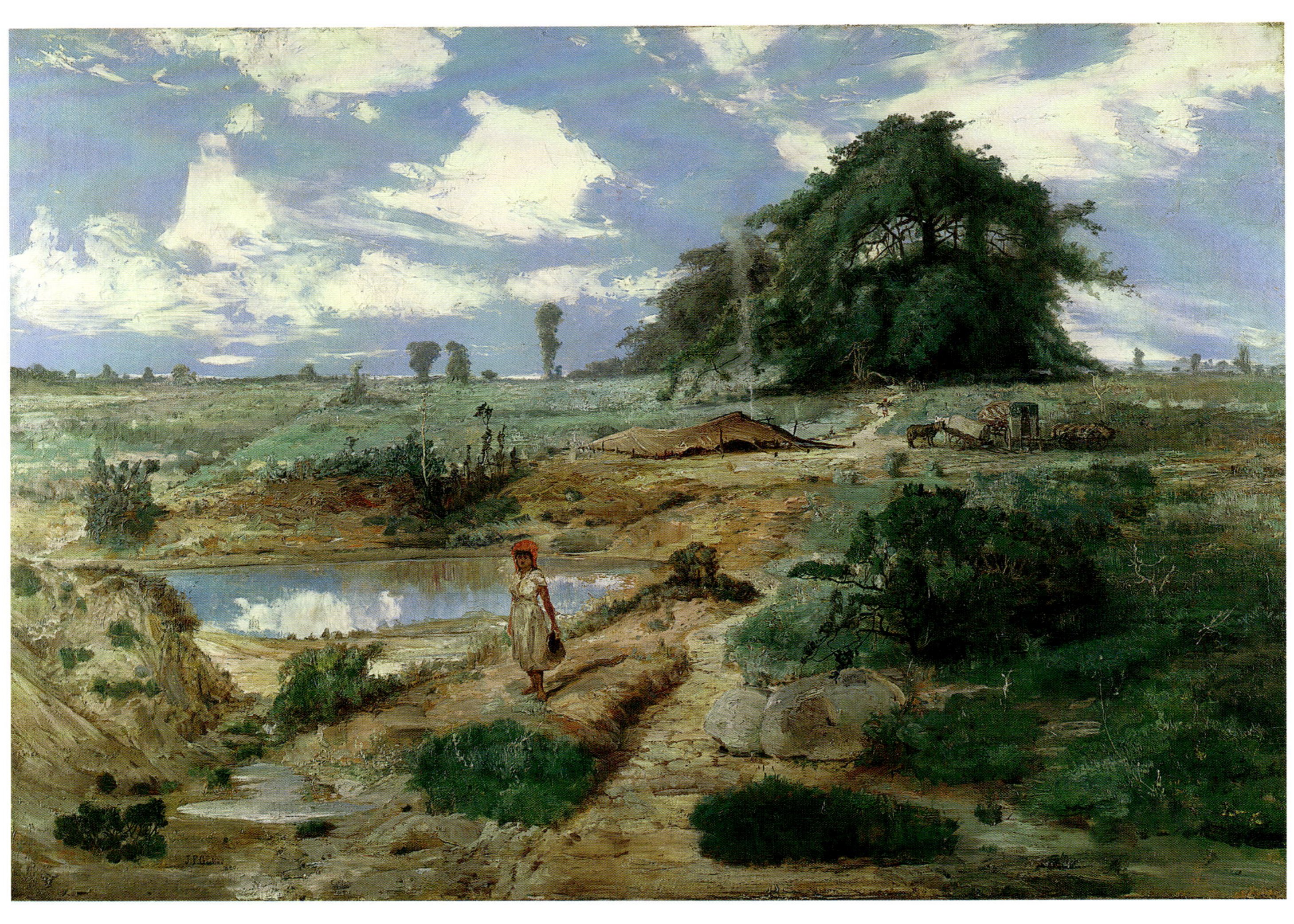

42. **James Farrington Gookins** (1840–1904)
Western Landscape, 1880, oil on canvas, 28 × 40 inches

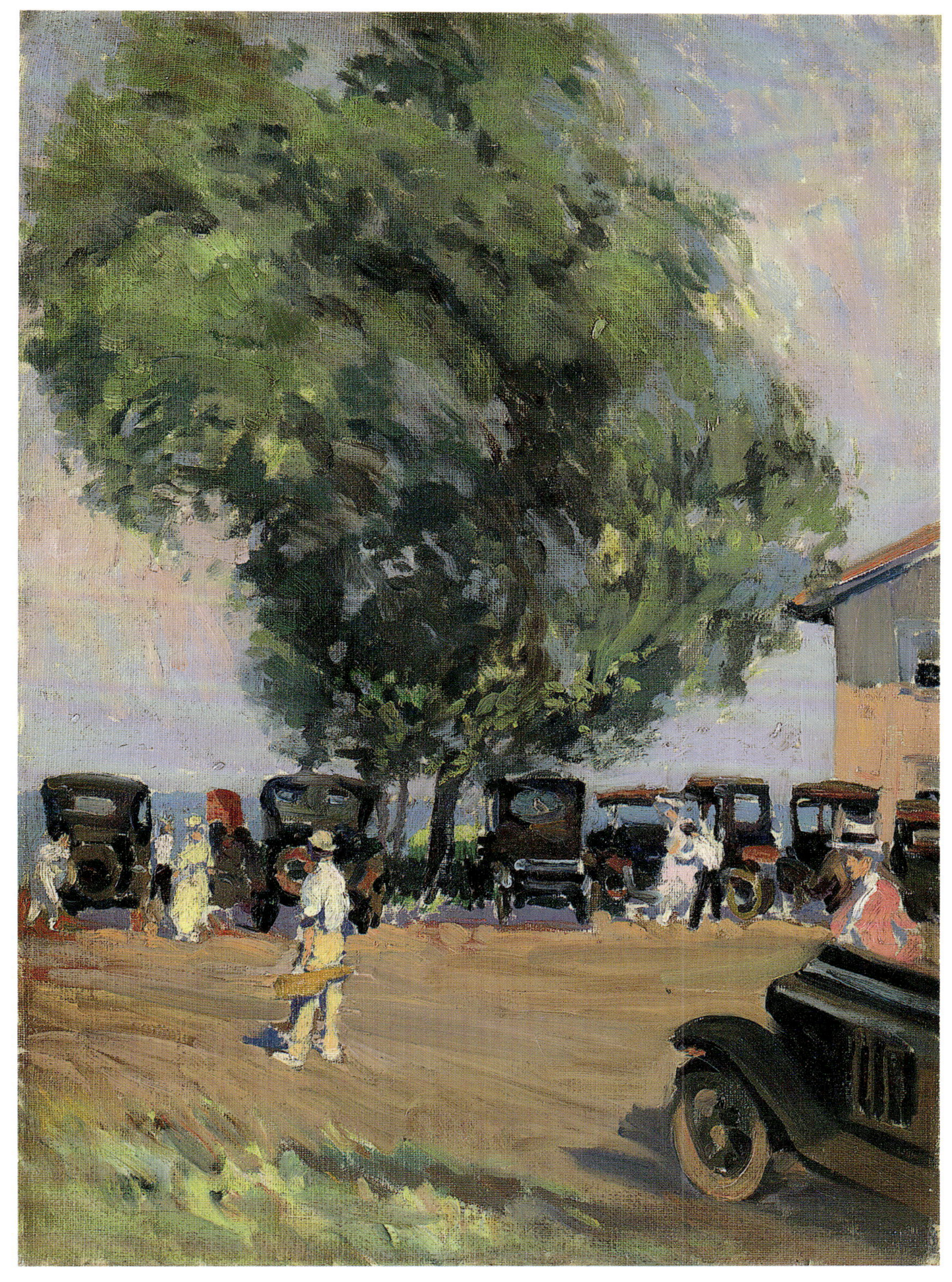

43. **Carl N. Werntz** (1874–1944)
Old Days, ca. 1910, oil on canvas, 20 × 14 inches

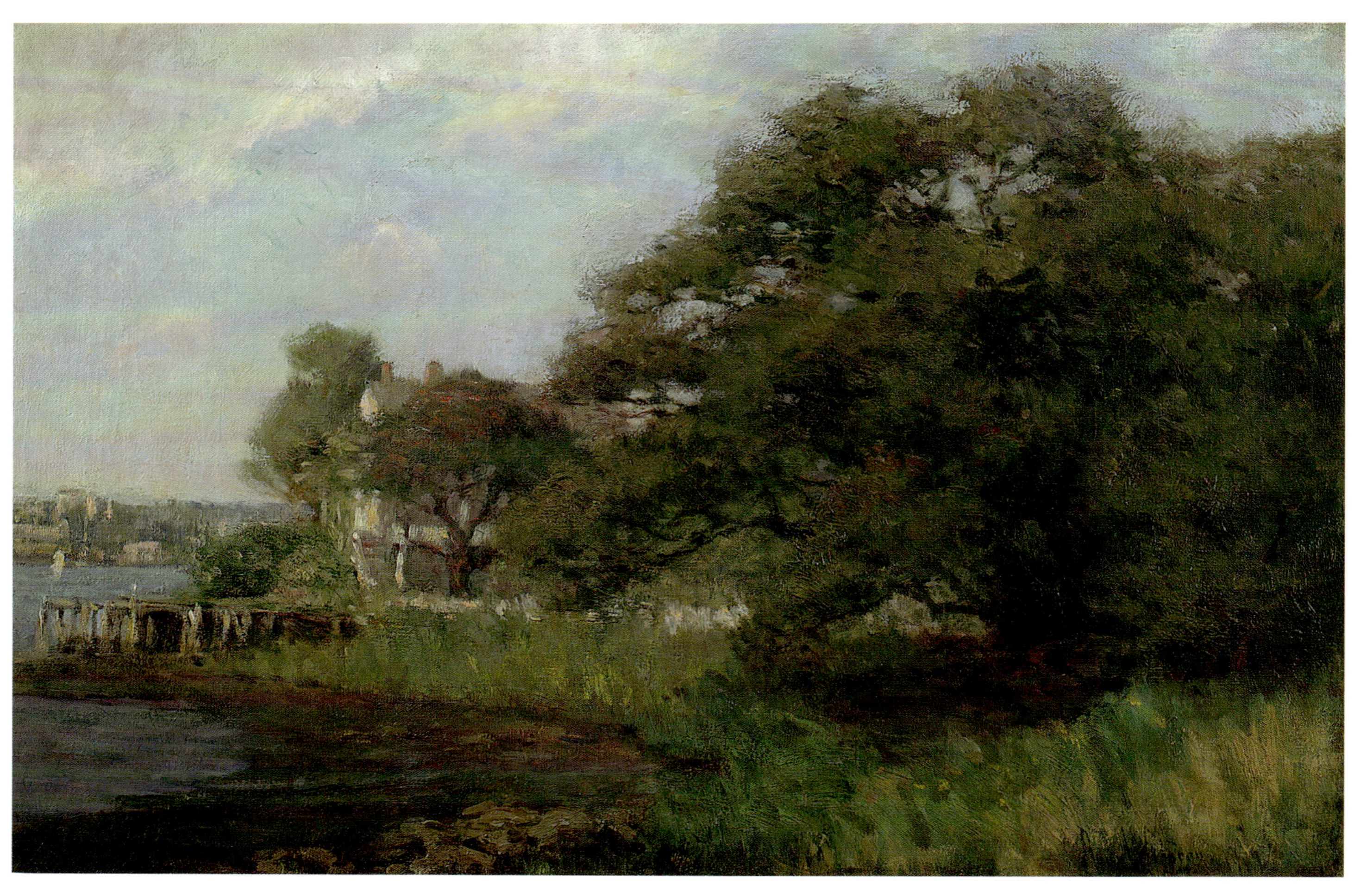

44. **Anna Lee Stacey** (1871–1943)
Willow, ca. 1919, oil on canvas, 16 × 24⅛ inches

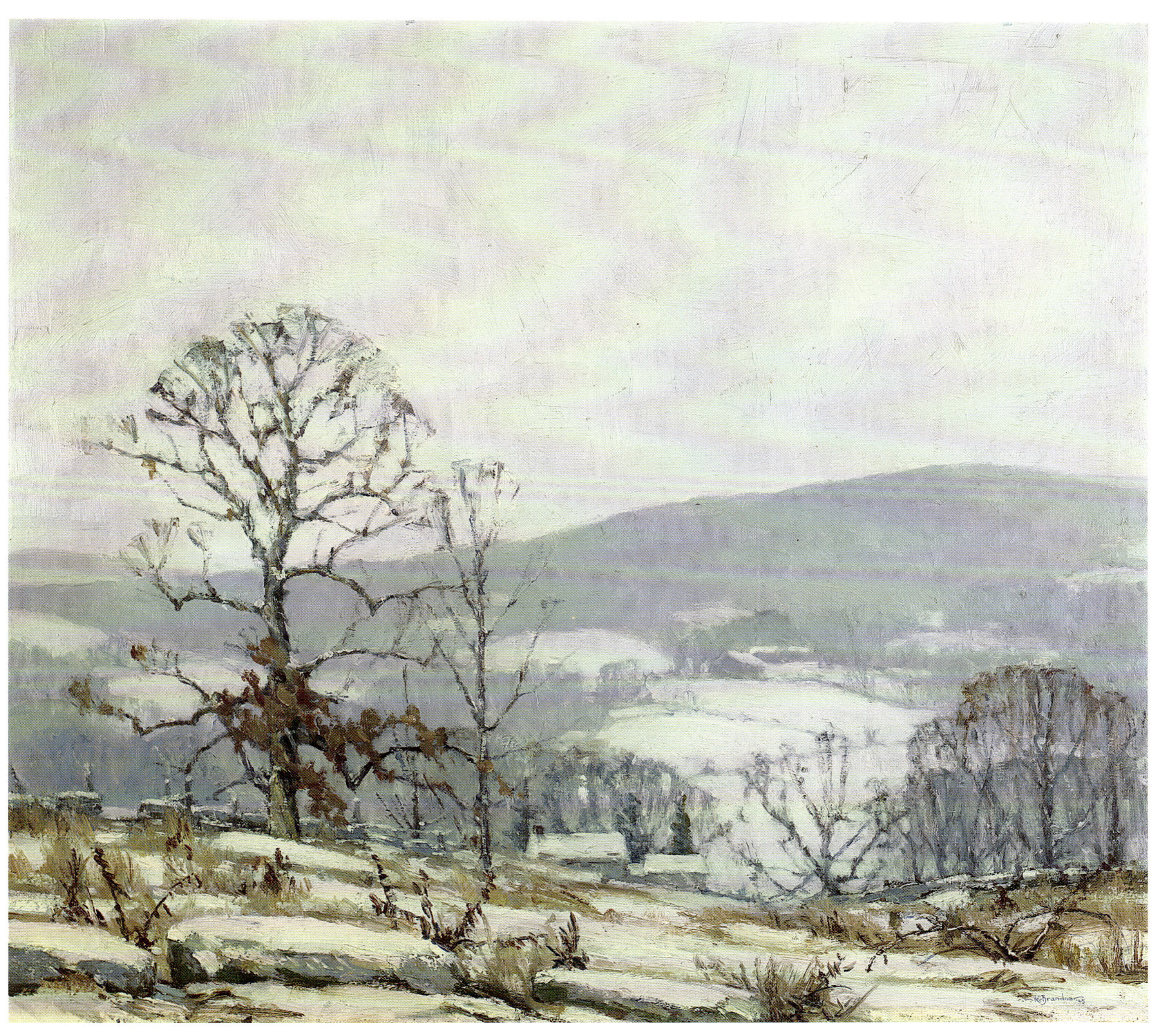

45. **Karl C. F. Brandner** (1898–1961)
Winter Landscape, ca. 1925, oil on board, 16¼ × 20 inches

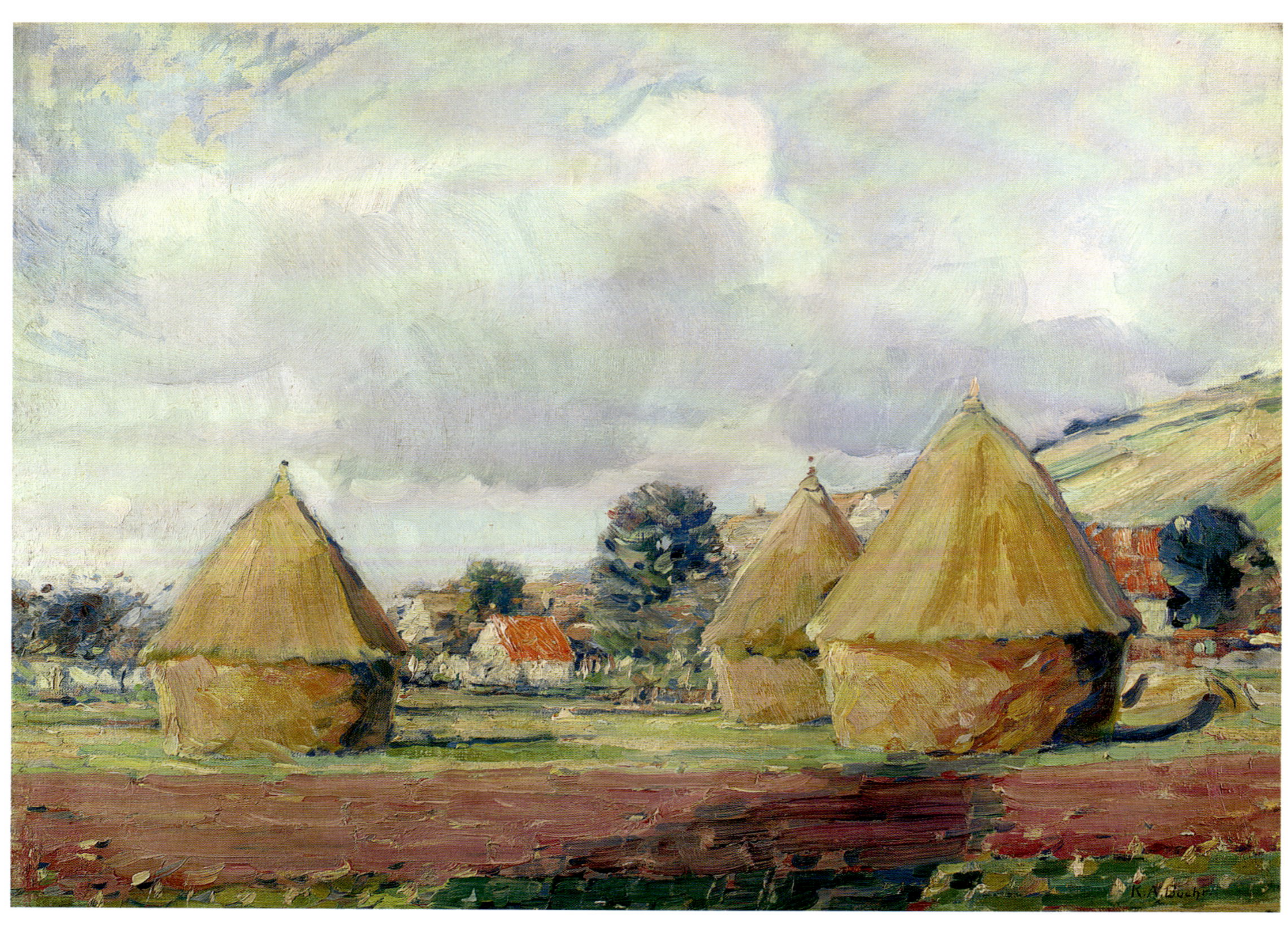

46. **Karl Buehr** (1866–1952)
The North Country (Haystacks), ca. 1910, oil on canvas, 20 × 28 inches

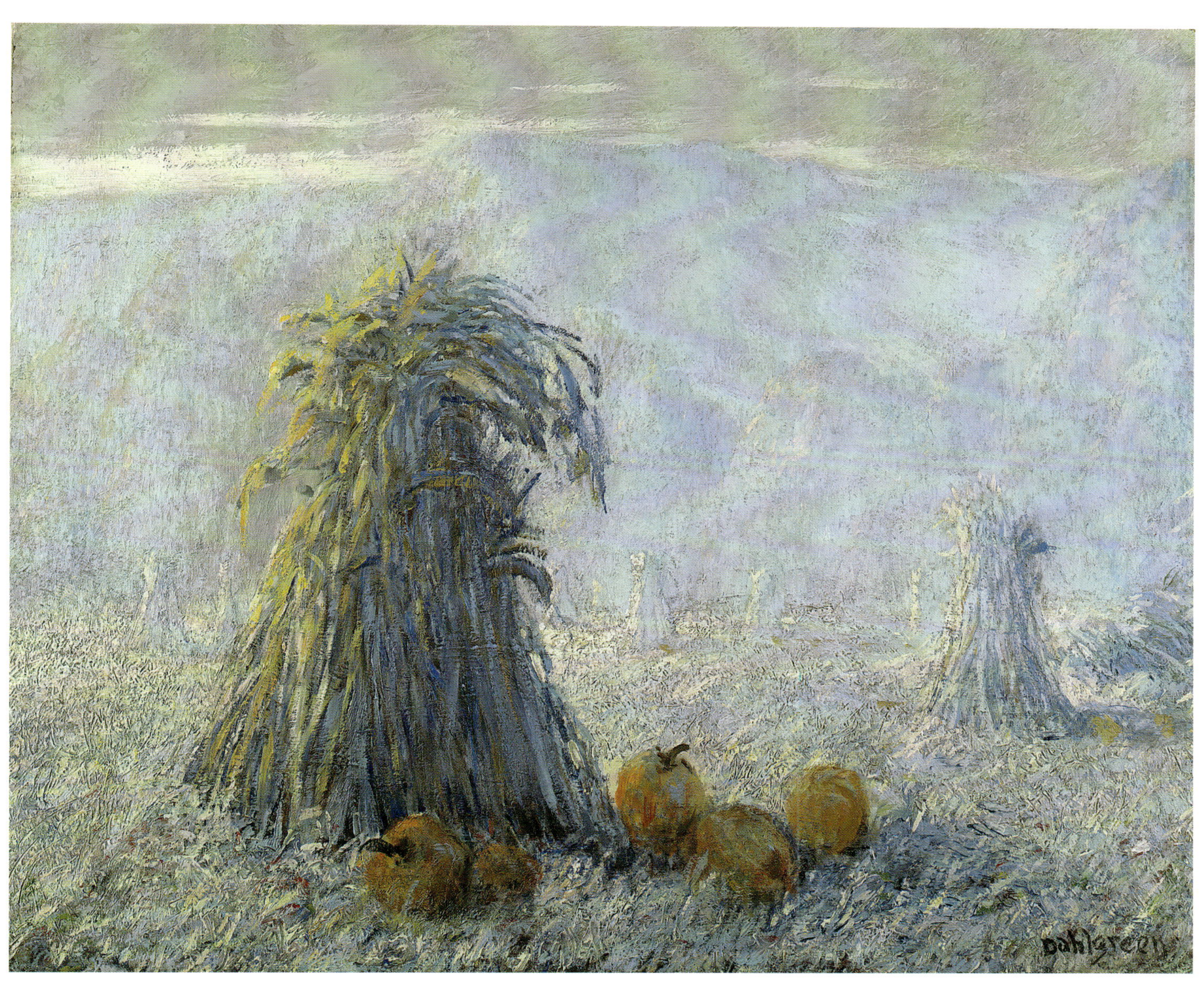

47. **Charles William Dahlgreen** (1864–1955)
Frosty Morning, ca. 1915, oil on canvas, 35 × 40 inches

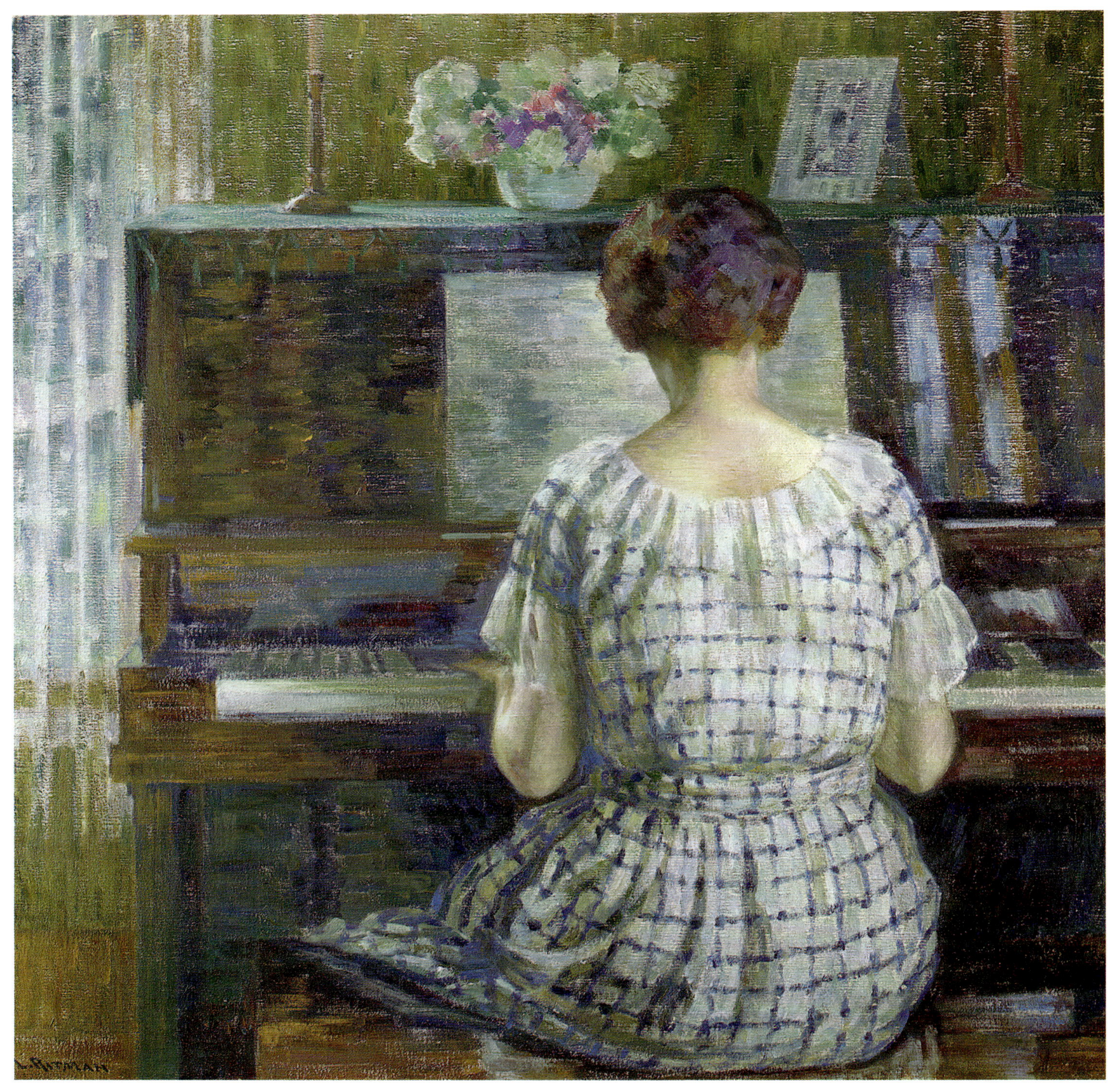

48. **Louis Ritman** (1889–1963)
At the Piano, ca. 1920, oil on canvas, 32 × 32 inches

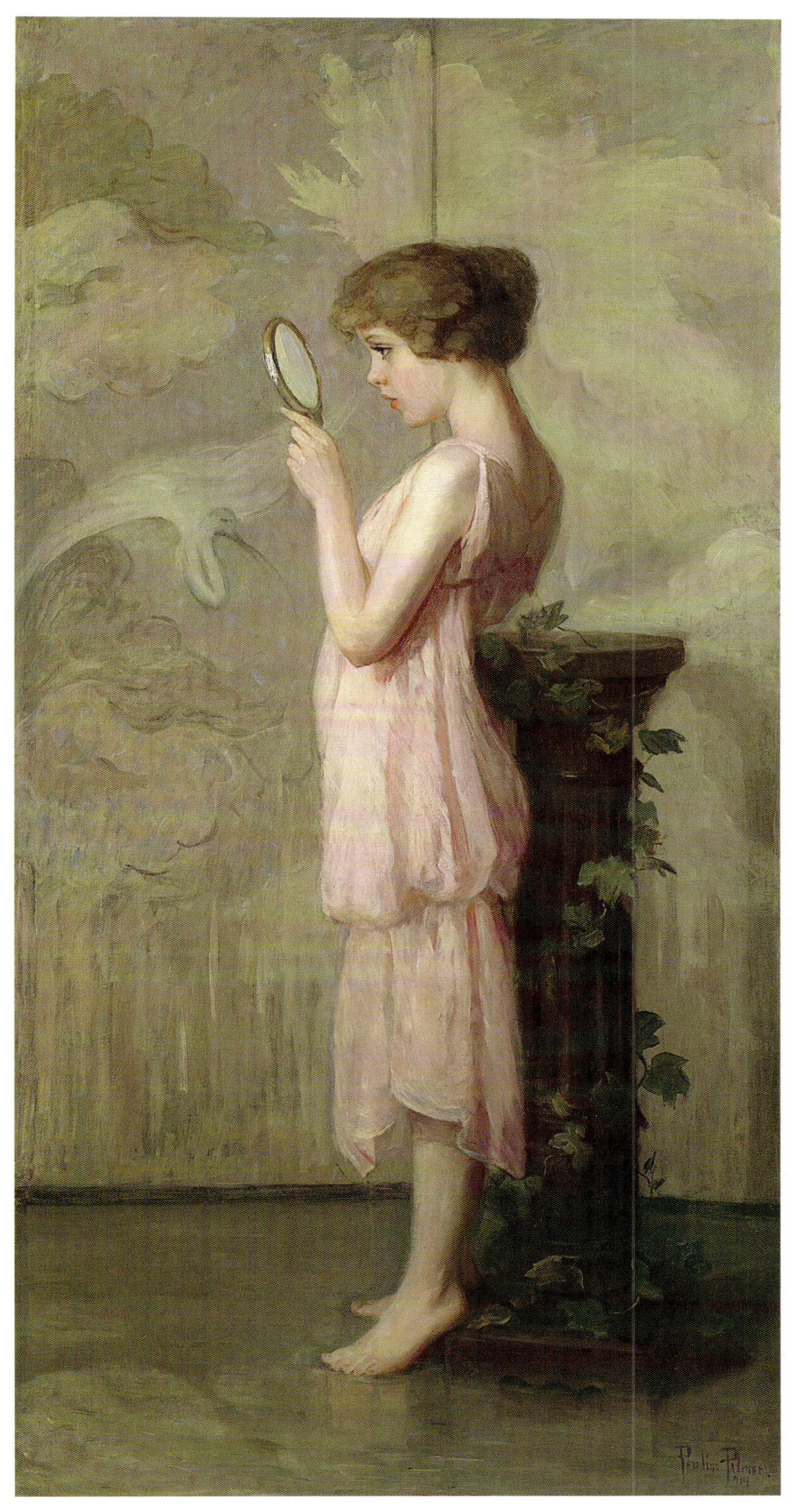

49. **Pauline Palmer** (1867–1938)
Patsy, ca. 1910, oil on canvas, 66 × 34 inches

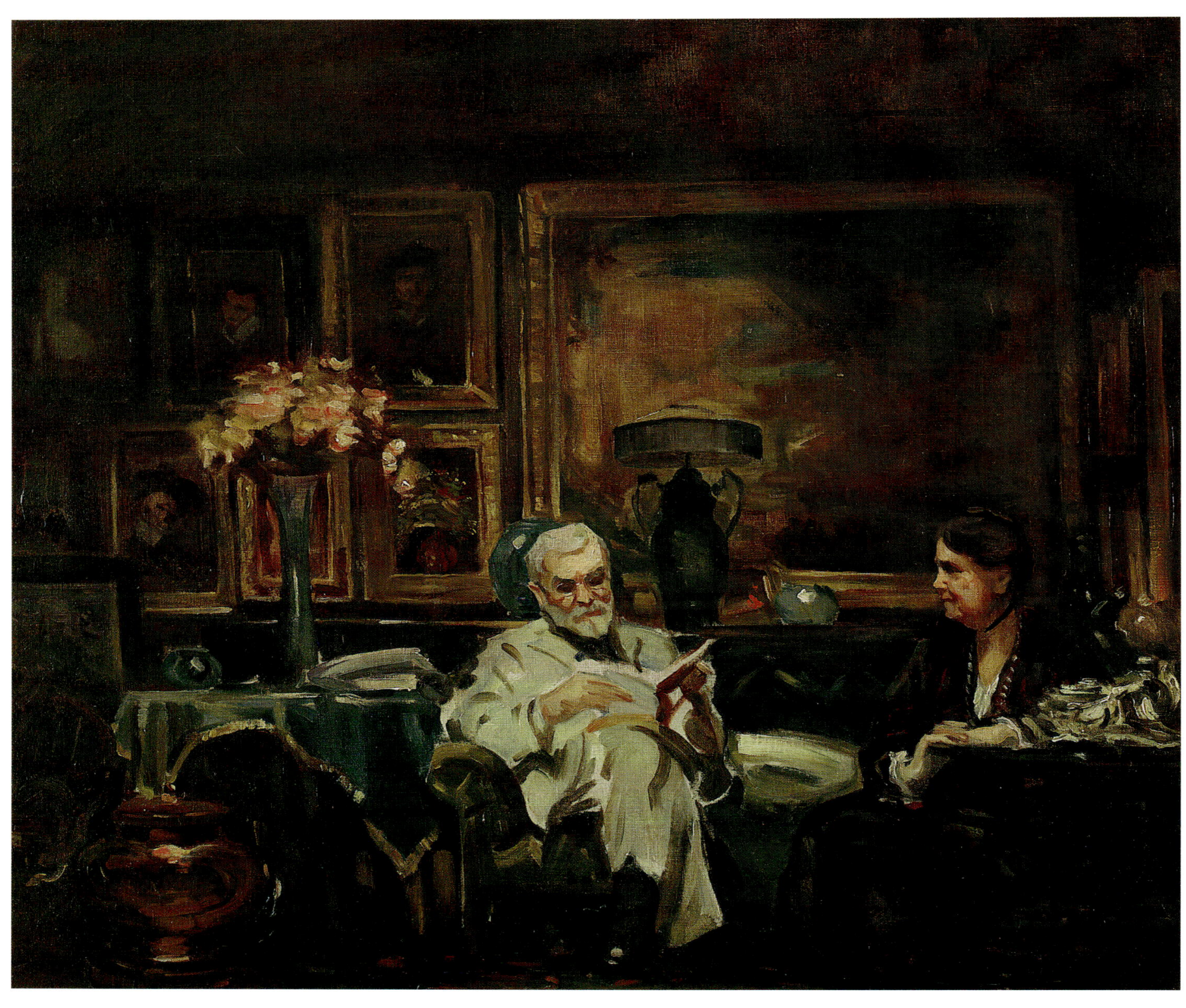

50. **John C. Johansen** (1876–1964)
The Collector (Mr. Robert Deforest and Wife), ca. 1915, oil on canvas, 30¼ × 35 inches

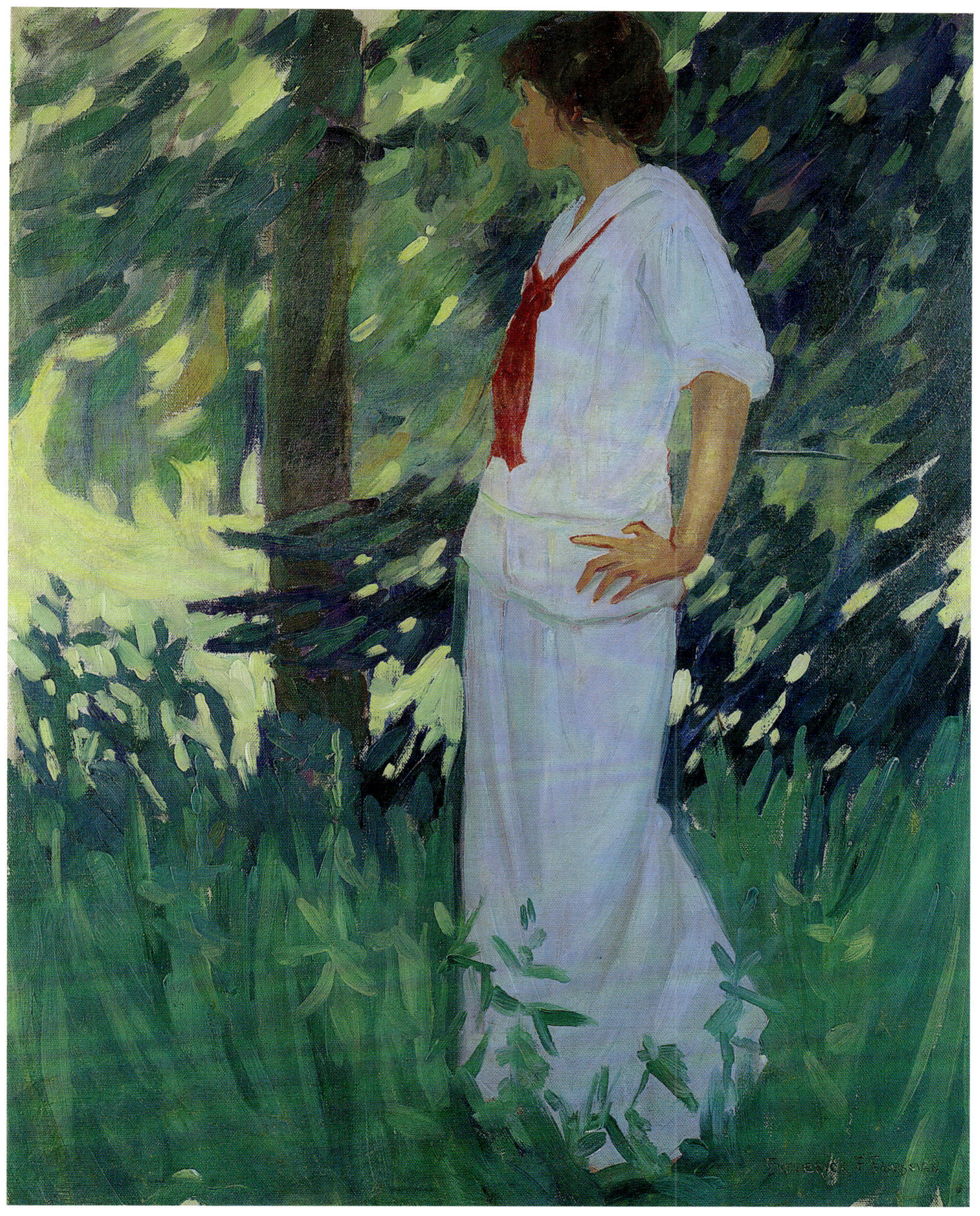

51. **Frederick Frary Fursman** (1874–1943)

Woman in Blue Middy, ca. 1910, oil on canvas, 29¾ × 23 inches

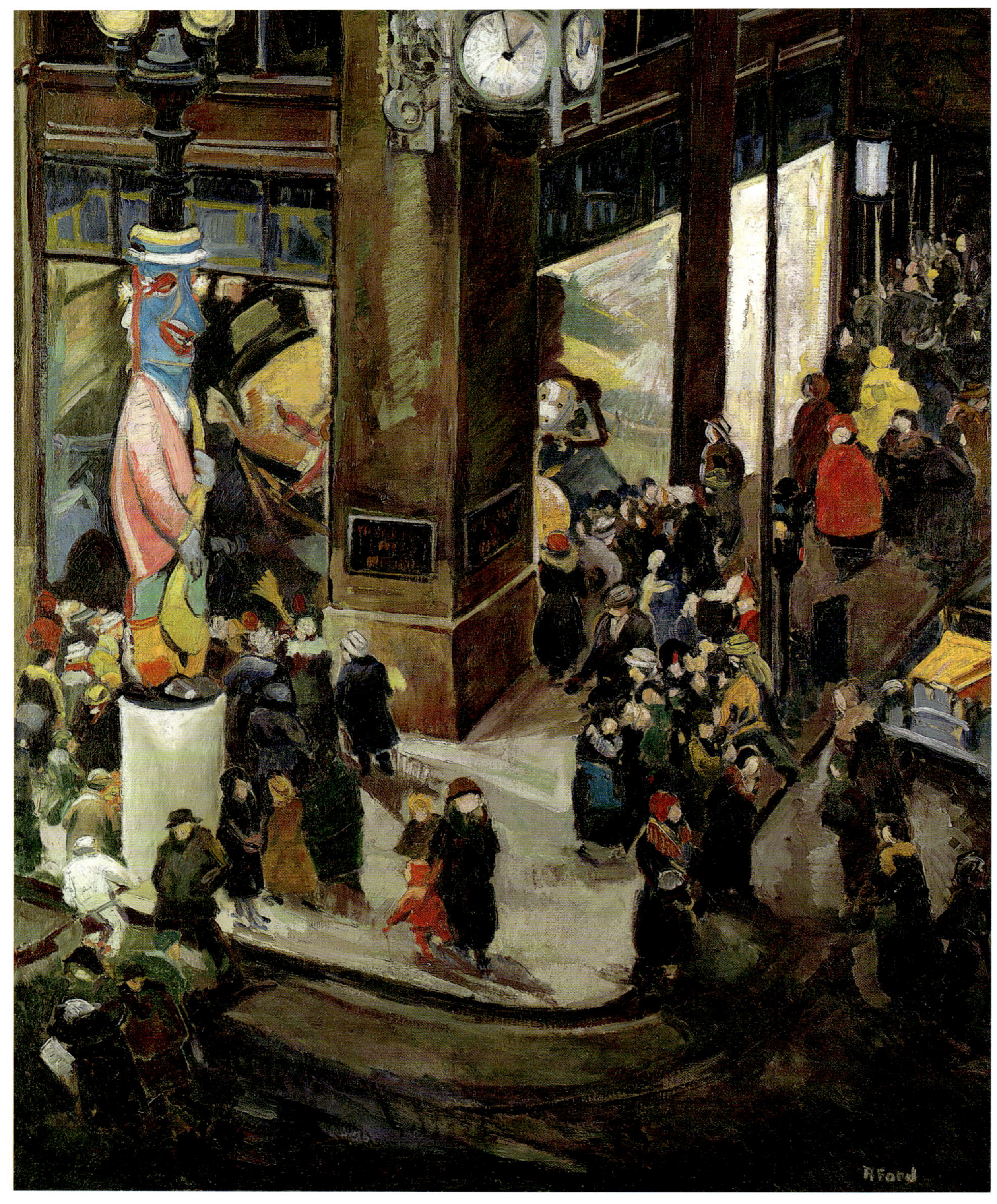

52. **Ruth Van Sickle Ford** (1897–1980)
State Street, ca. 1931, oil on canvas, 58 × 40 inches

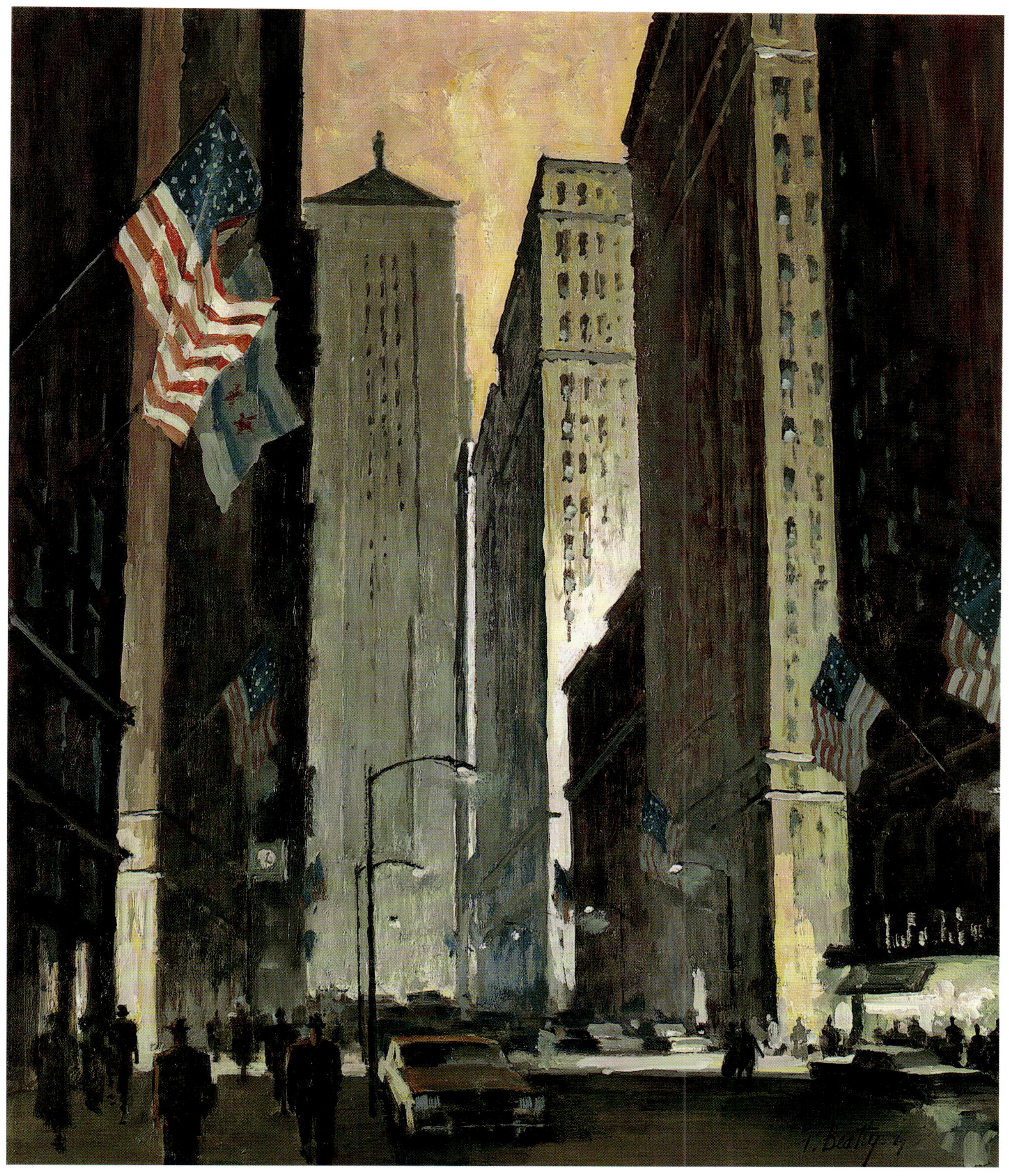

53. **Frank T. Moore Beatty** (1900–active in 1984)
LaSalle Street, 1967, oil on canvas, 40 × 24 inches

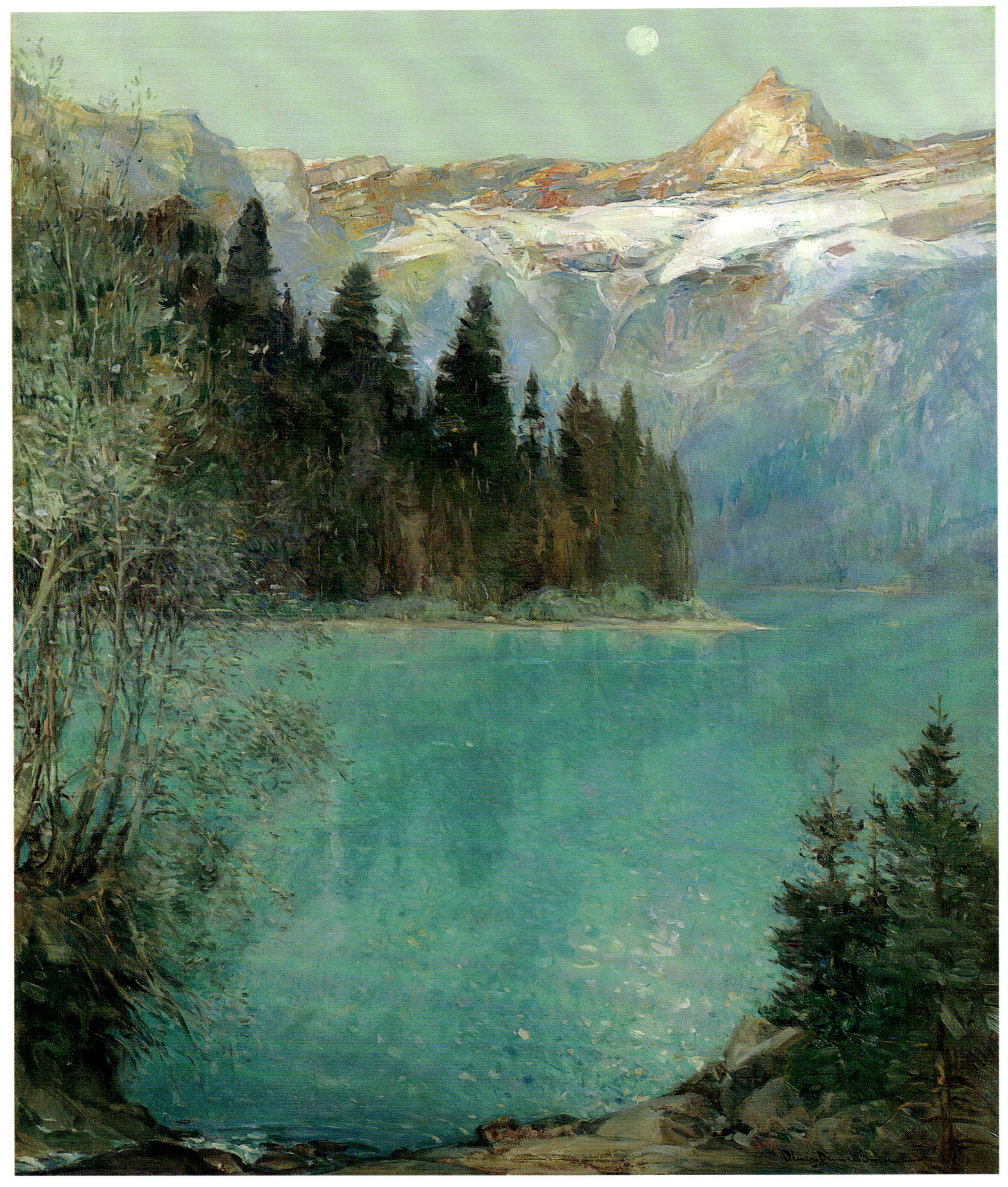

54. **Oliver Dennett Grover** (1860–1927)
Avalanche Lake, ca. 1920s, oil on canvas, 48 × 36 inches

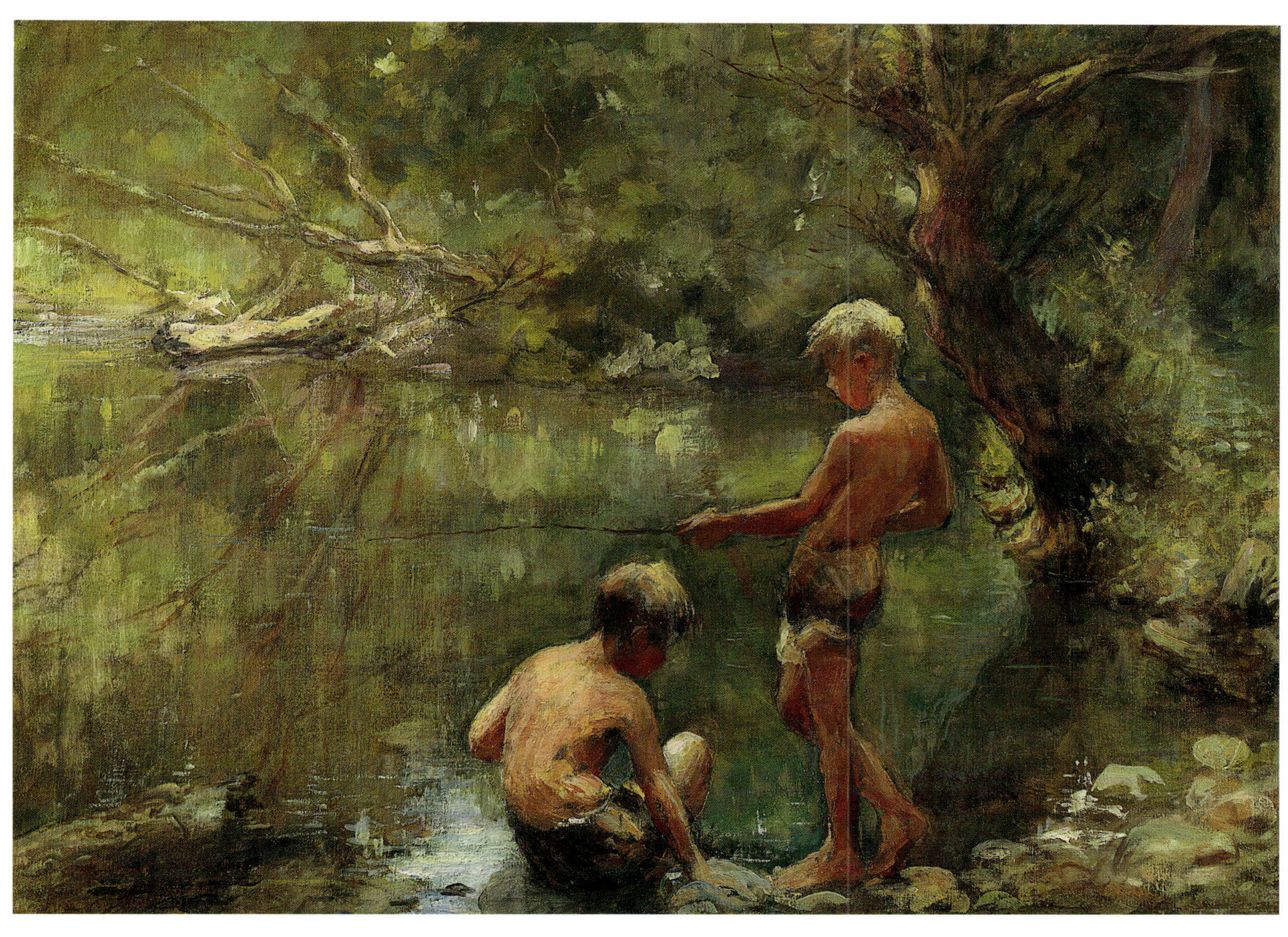

55. **Adam Emory Albright** (1862–1957)
Two Boys Fishing (Ivan and Malvin Albright), 1908, oil on canvas, 26¼ × 36½ inches

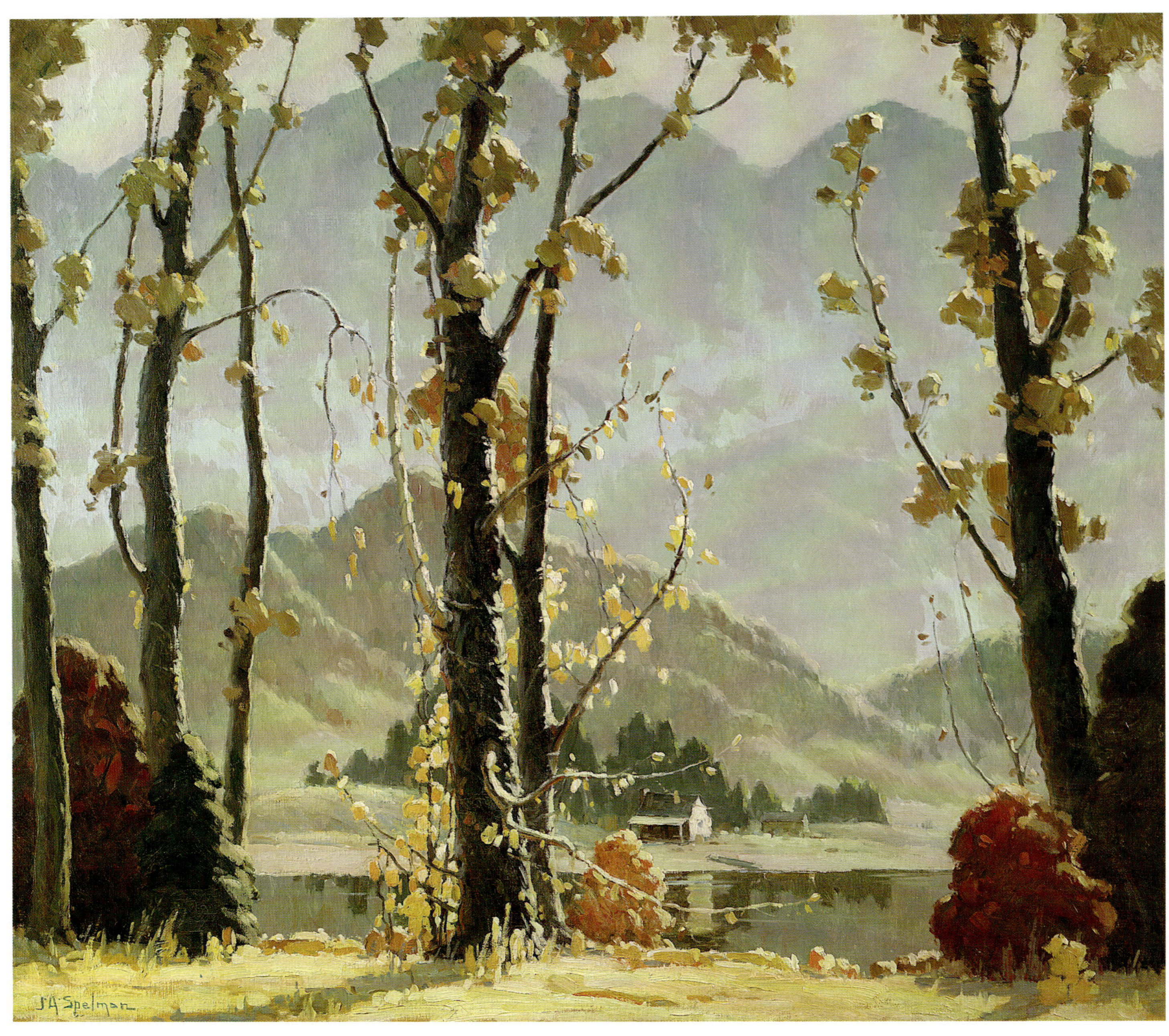

56. **John Adams Spelman** (1880–1941)
North Carolina Mountain Landscape, ca. 1926, oil on canvas, 32 × 36 inches

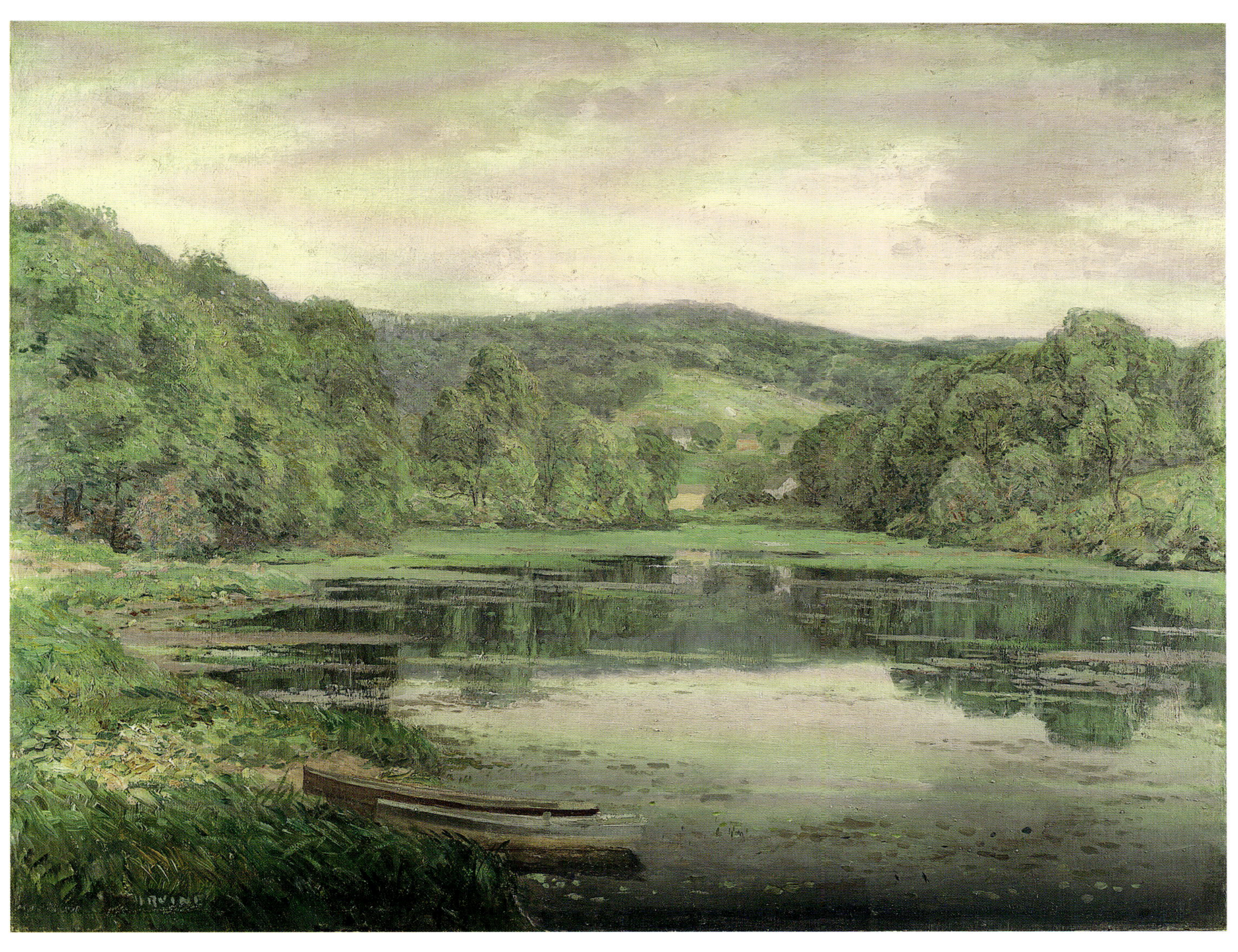

57. **Wilson Henry Irvine** (1869–1936)
Old Lyme Pond, ca. 1918, oil on canvas, 30 × 40 inches

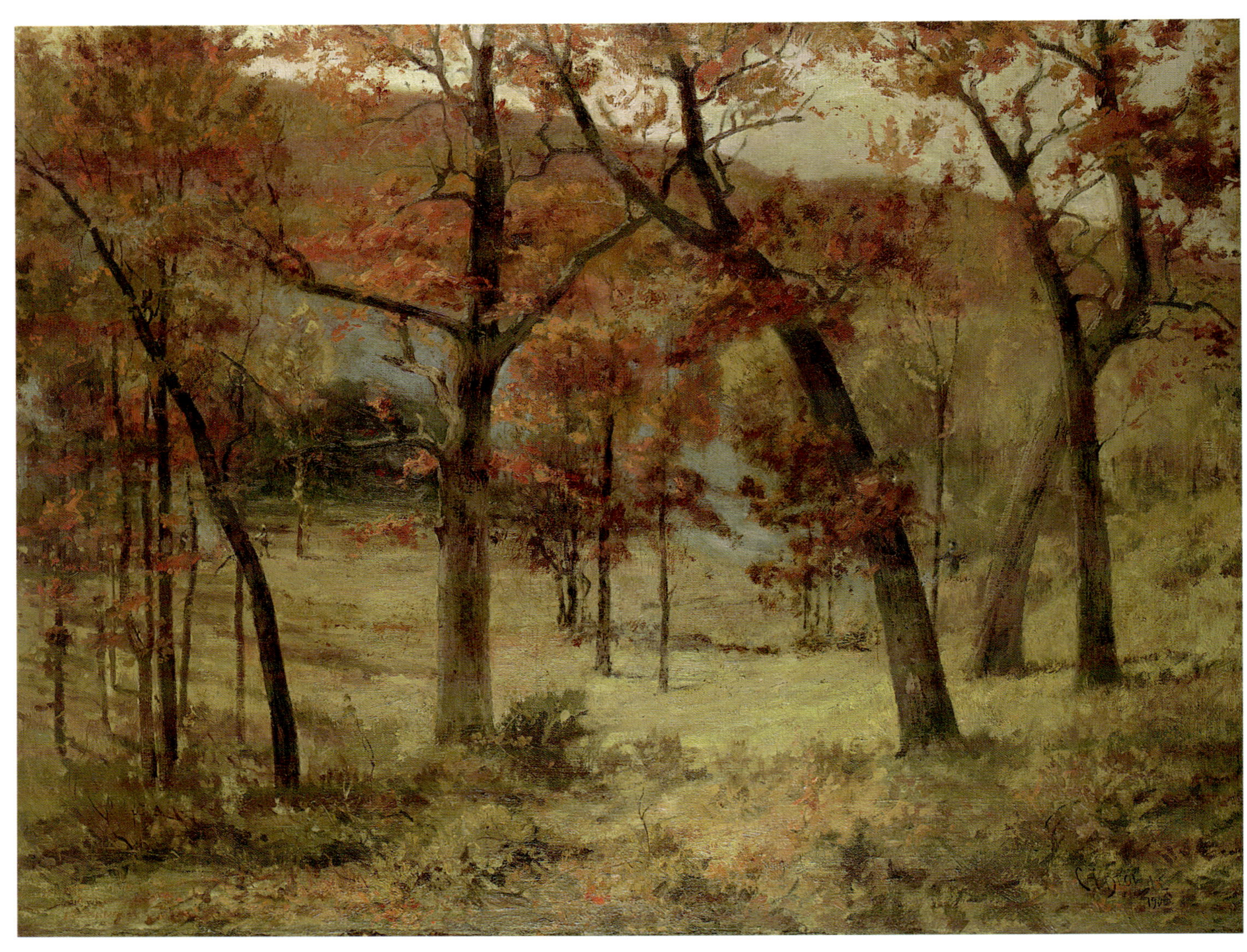

58. **Charles Francis Browne** (1859–1920)
The Clearing, 1906, oil on board, 36 × 47 inches

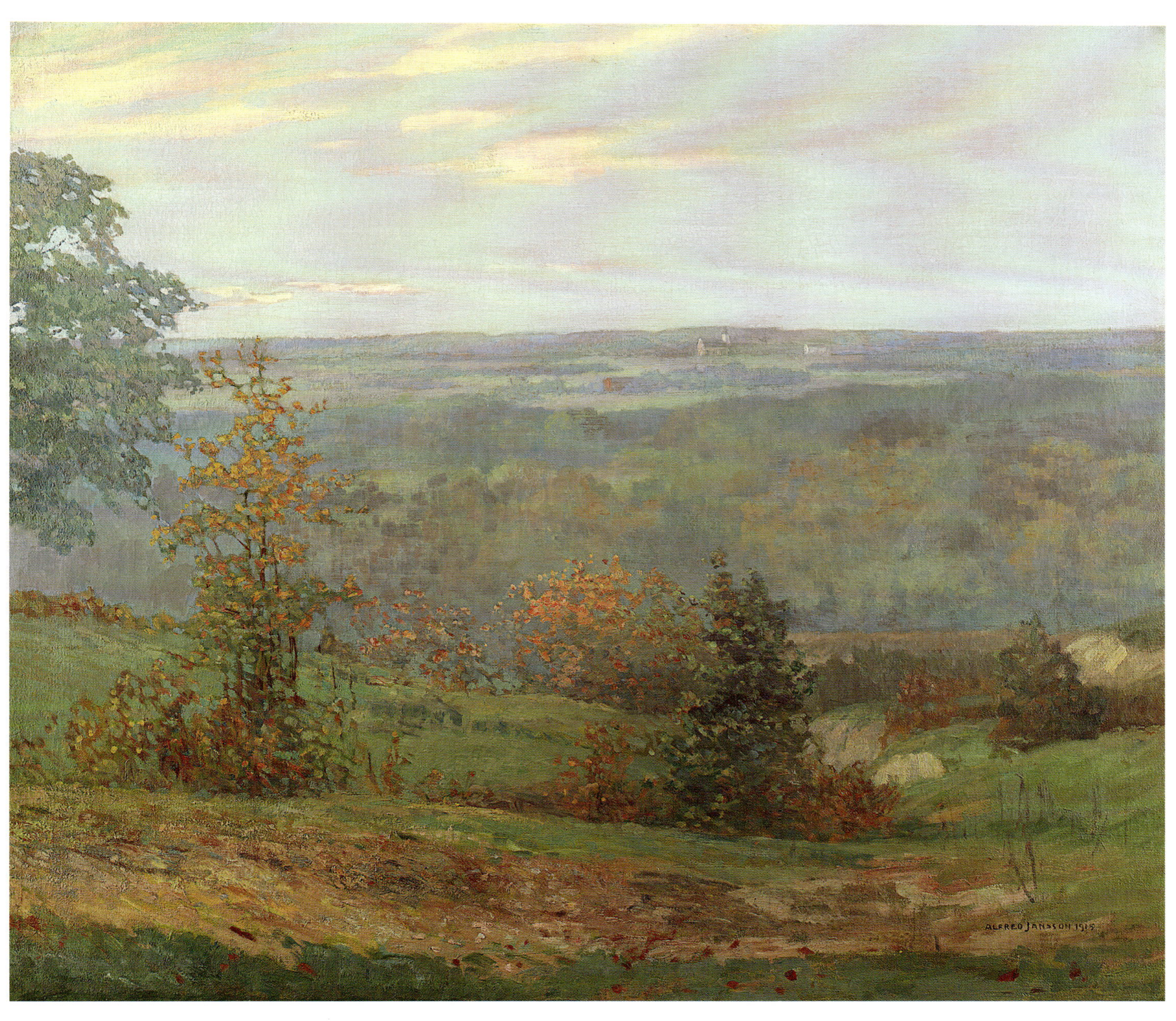

59. **Alfred Jansson** (1863–1931)
Fall Landscape, Galena, 1915, oil on canvas, 33¼ × 38 inches

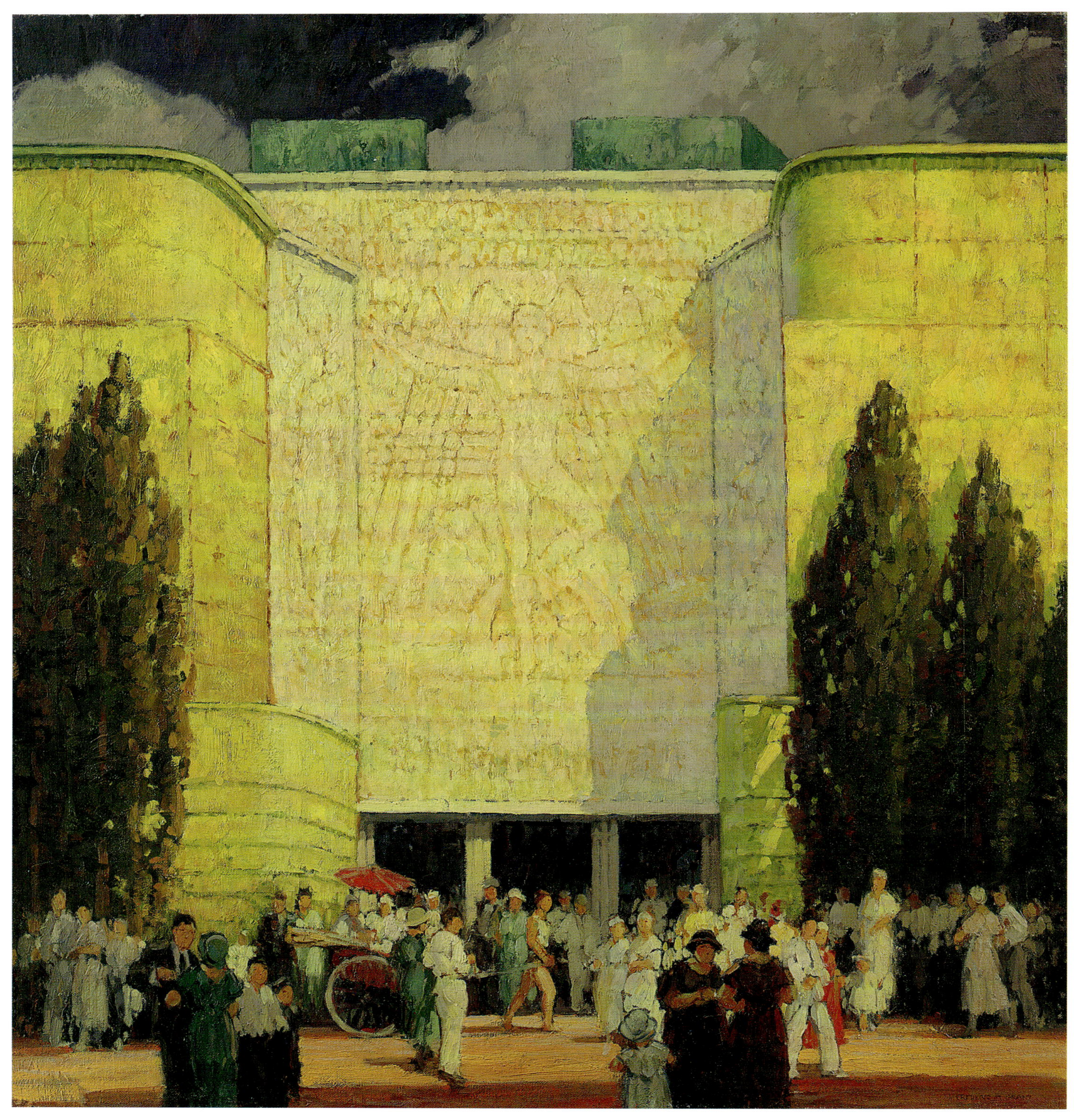

60. **Frederic Milton Grant** (1886–1959)
*Entrance to Western Union Hall, Century of Progress International
Exposition, Chicago*, ca. 1933, oil on canvas, 33 × 31 inches

BIOGRAPHIES

Gerda-Maria Ahlm (1869–1956)

Little is known of the life and career of Gerda-Maria Ahlm, a landscape and portrait painter who was born in Vesteros, Sweden. The artist studied at the Royal Academy of Stockholm as well as at art academies in Paris and Rome. By 1905 she had settled in Chicago. She exhibited at the Art Institute of Chicago (1905 and 1906) and was a member of the Society of Swedish Artists, Stockholm.

Adam Emory Albright (1862–1957)

Adam Emory Albright painted many landscapes, but his reputation was based primarily on his depictions of rural children frolicking in outdoor settings. Born in Monroe, Wisconsin, he studied at the School of the Art Institute of Chicago and with Thomas Eakins at the Pennsylvania Academy of the Fine Arts in Philadelphia before going to Europe in 1887 for additional training in Munich and Paris. In 1888 he established his studio in Chicago and painted landscapes, portraits, the occasional still life, and eventually, children; his ability to translate the essence of childhood into paint earned him a reputation as the "James Whitcomb Riley of the Brush"—Riley (1849–1916) was an Indiana poet noted for his colorful descriptions of Hoosier life. Beginning in 1908 Albright spent summers at the Brown County art colony in Indiana. He was well known to Chicagoans, who could see his paintings at the annual exhibitions of the Art Institute from 1896 until 1939, and at other local venues. After 1917 he spent his winters in Arizona, California, and South America, where he painted desert landscapes and figural subjects. In addition to his activity as an easel painter, the artist operated the Albright Atelier in Lamar, Missouri. He died in Warrenville, Illinois, in 1957.

George Ames Aldrich (1872–1941)

A talented landscape painter and etcher, George Ames Aldrich was born in Worcester, Massachusetts. During the 1890s, while living abroad, he worked as an illustrator for the *London Times* and *Punch*. He received his formal training at the Art Students League in New York and at the Massachusetts Institute of Technology, Cambridge, where he may have studied architecture. He also took classes in Paris, at the Académies Julian and Colarossi and at the Académie Carmen, where he was taught by James McNeill Whistler. During his years in France, which included a sojourn in Dieppe during 1909–10, he produced some of his finest works—landscapes and village scenes painted in Normandy and Brittany. Aldrich made Chicago his home in 1918 and for many years was active in the art scene in South Bend, Indiana. He exhibited romantic depictions of Indiana dune country at the annuals of the Art Institute of Chicago as well as views of France and Cape Ann, Massachusetts. In 1924 he traveled back to Europe, spending six months at the American Academy in Rome, three months at the Fontainebleau School of Fine Arts in France, and painting and sketching throughout Italy, France, Spain, Germany, and England. Aldrich died in Chicago in 1941.

Frank T. Moore Beatty (1900 – active in 1984)

Frank T. Moore Beatty was a painter of cityscapes and industrial landscapes, active in Chicago in the early and mid-twentieth century. He was born in Winnipeg, Manitoba, and studied at the Winnipeg School of Art (1917–24). After settling in Chicago in 1924, he created oils, pastels, and watercolors, depicting harbors, boats, landscapes, industrial buildings, and street scenes. He found his subjects in and around Chicago as well as in New York, Mexico, Puerto Rico, and Florida. Beatty also worked as a commercial artist for *Popular Mechanics Magazine* and produced graphic designs and prints. He exhibited at the Art Institute of Chicago in 1931, and his work is included in the collection of the Telfair Museum of Art, Savannah, Georgia.

Harold Betts (1883–1963)

The painter and illustrator Harold Betts was born in New York City. He received his artistic training from his father, the painter Edwin Daniel Betts, Sr., who also taught his siblings, Grace, Louis, and E. D. Betts, Jr. Betts lived in Chicago, studied at the School of the Art Institute, and exhibited oils and watercolors intermittently at the institute annuals from 1897 to 1931. His oeuvre consists of landscapes painted in Michigan, Maine, Florida, and Louisiana. He also painted views of the Grand Canyon and Pueblo Indian themes inspired by trips to the Southwest. Betts exhibited twenty-three works at the Hackley Art Gallery in Muskegon, Michigan, in 1929.

Daniel Folger Bigelow (1823–1910)

Hailing from Peru in New York state, Daniel Folger Bigelow became one of Chicago's most prominent painters of landscapes and still lifes. Although largely self-taught, he received some art instruction from Asahel Powers, a portrait painter and cousin of the sculptor Hiram Powers. After supporting himself at first by painting portraits and working in a marble quarry, Bigelow moved to Chicago in 1858. For the next five decades he specialized in landscape painting, working in both oil and watercolor, while also executing a number of still lifes. The material for his pictures came from his summer sketching trips to Wisconsin and to the shores of Lake Michigan. He frequently traveled back to New York and toured all of New England as well. The paintings from his excursions found a ready market among Chicago patrons with eastern roots, some of whom commissioned pictures of particular scenes and locales. Bigelow's art reveals a delicacy of color and treatment and an earnest naturalism indebted to the Hudson River School artists. During the 1890s and the rise of American Impressionism, the artist lightened his palette and began using more vivid colors, as well as showing greater interest in atmospheric effects.

Karl C. F. Brandner (1898–1961)

A native of Chicago, Karl C. F. Brandner was both a landscape painter and a printmaker. Although discouraged by his family from pursuing a career in art, he studied at the School of the Art Institute of Chicago during the early 1920s. Operating a rotogravure press, Brandner supported himself by working for various newspapers and printing companies while continuing to paint and draw. He also produced etchings and art prints. He later lived in Detroit for five years and attended the Detroit School of Art while working for the *Detroit News*. When Brandner first exhibited his paintings at the Art Institute of Chicago in 1927, the critics praised their technical accomplishment and naturalistic orientation. He eventually developed a broader, looser style, subtle coloring, and a strong interest in the effects of light. From 1929 until 1955 Brandner exhibited his work almost annually at Chicago's Hoosier Salon, a forum in which he won numerous prizes and awards, particularly during the 1930s.

Charles Francis Browne (1859–1920)

A Chicago-based landscape painter, teacher, and critic, Charles Francis Browne was born in Natick, Massachusetts. He worked in a lithographic firm and took classes at the Boston Museum School prior to enrolling in 1885 at the Pennsylvania Academy of the Fine Arts, Philadelphia, where he spent the next two years studying under Thomas Eakins. After further training with Abbott Thayer in Boston and Jean-Léon Gérôme in France, he settled in Chicago about 1892. He subsequently taught at the School of the Art Institute and painted landscapes in Illinois, especially in and around Oregon. He was also active as a writer, reviewing art exhibitions for the *Chicago Sunday Tribune* and editing the art journal *Brush and Pencil*. Along with the writer Hamlin Garland and the sculptor Lorado Taft, he produced the influential pamphlet *Impressions on Impressionism* (1894), which signaled the growing interest in that aesthetic. Browne himself painted in a conservative Tonalist style, but after the turn of the century he incorporated Impressionist strategies into his work. A 1904 trip to France and to Scotland, where he encountered the paintings of the Glasgow School, were important to his later predilection for soft colors, generalized forms, and the effects of light and atmosphere.

Karl Buehr (1866–1952)

A noted figure and landscape painter who was much admired for his skills as a colorist, Karl Buehr was born in Feverbach, Germany. After studying intermittently at the School of the Art Institute of Chicago from 1888 to 1897, and with the painter Frank Duveneck in 1899, he continued his training abroad, attending classes at the Académies Julian and Colarossi in Paris before enrolling at the London Art School in 1903. He returned to Paris in 1908. From 1909 until 1911 Buehr and his wife, the miniature painter Mary Hess Buehr, lived in the artists' colony in Giverny, France. There he began portraying female models—often dressed in nineteenth-century gowns—in the open air, employing the decorative Impressionist style favored by Frederick Frieseke, Richard Miller, and other American figure painters working in Giverny during the early 1900s. Buehr was active in the town of Sainte-Geneviève, near Giverny, about 1912 to 1913, after which time he returned to Chicago. Thereafter, he taught for many years at the Art Institute while spending his summers painting landscapes and interior figural subjects in Wyoming, New York.

Theodore Earl Butler (1861–1936)

An important member of the Impressionist artists' colony in Giverny, France, at the turn of the last century, Theodore Earl Butler was one of only a few American painters to have direct contact with Claude Monet. Butler, a painter of figural subjects and landscapes, developed a distinctive style based on a synthesis of Impressionist and Post-Impressionist precepts. In Paris, his work was championed by such dealers as Ambrose Vollard and Paul Durand-Ruel. Born in Columbus, Ohio, Butler studied at the Art Students League in New York and at the Académies Julian, Colarossi, and the Grande Chaumière in Paris. He visited Giverny in 1888, 1890, and 1891, experimenting with modern strategies of light and color. He became a permanent resident of the village in 1892, when he married Suzanne Hoschedé, Monet's stepdaughter. In the ensuing years, Butler evolved his mature style, adopting a high-keyed palette and expressionistic brushwork that he applied to genre scenes of his wife and children. In 1900, following Suzanne's death in 1899, Butler married her sister Marthe. He went back to New York in 1913, spending the next eight years executing mural commissions and painting urban scenes before returning permanently to Giverny, where he died.

Edgar S. Cameron (1862–1944)

A painter of landscapes, portraits, and figural subjects, Edgar S. Cameron was born in Ottawa, Illinois. He studied at the Chicago Academy of Design and the Chicago Academy of Fine Arts before going in 1882 to New York, where he resumed his training at the Art Students League with William Merritt Chase and Thomas Wilmer Dewing. From 1883 to 1890 he lived primarily in Paris, studying at the Académies Julian and Colarossi and at the Ecole des Beaux-Arts. Returning to Chicago, he became an art critic for the *Chicago Tribune*, in which capacity he reviewed local exhibitions, including the progressive art shown at the World's Columbian Exposition of 1893. During an extended trip to France (1893–96), he refined his skills at the Académie Julian in Paris and made painting trips to the countryside. He went abroad again in 1900 and during 1911–13. In addition to portraying European scenery, Cameron painted landscapes in Illinois and Michigan, as well as in Santa Fe, New Mexico, which he visited in 1917. Beginning in 1891 he was a regular contributor to the Art Institute of Chicago's annual exhibitions, where he won many prizes. He had solo exhibitions at the Art Institute in 1909 and 1924, at the Chicago Art Galleries Association in 1929, and at the All-Illinois Society of Fine Arts in 1930. His "moonlight pictures" were among his most popular works.

Francis Chapin (1899–1965)

A respected figure in Chicago art circles during the 1930s and 1940s, Francis Chapin worked in a modernist style that blended the real and the abstract. Born in Bristolville, Ohio, he attended Washington and Jefferson College in Pennsylvania, receiving a bachelor of science degree in 1921. A year later he moved to Chicago, taking classes at the School of the Art Institute until 1928, when he went to Europe to familiarize himself with contemporary art there. Returning to Chicago in 1929, Chapin had one-man shows at the Art Institute and at the galleries of Carson, Pirie, Scott, and Company. The following year, he joined the Art Institute's faculty as an instructor of painting and lithography. His painting oeuvre includes views of Europe as well as still lifes and the occasional figure subject. Like many artists of his milieu, he also portrayed the American Scene—in his case, the streets, alleys, and dilapidated houses of Chicago's North Side. From 1926 to 1951 Chapin was a regular contributor to the Art Institute's annual exhibitions, where he won a number of prestigious awards. He also exhibited inter-mittently in the East, winning such honors as the National Academy of Design's Hallgarten Prize (1930) and the Sesnan Medal at the Pennsylvania Academy of the Fine Arts (1939).

Charles William Dahlgreen (1864–1955)

Charles William Dahlgreen was one of Chicago's most promi-nent and versatile artists of the first half of the twentieth cen-tury. Although he specialized in landscape painting, he was also a master printmaker, producing etchings and drypoints of landscape subjects. A Chicago native, Dahlgreen became interested in art at an early age and studied in Düsseldorf in 1886–88. On his return, however, he went into business for over fifteen years creating painted and embroidered flags and banners. About 1904, feeling financially secure, he enrolled in the Chicago Academy of Fine Arts and later attended the School of Art Institute of Chicago. After graduating from the institute in 1909, Dahlgreen spent the next two years in Europe, copying old master paintings in England, Belgium, Holland, France, and Italy. On returning to Chicago, he even-tually settled in nearby Oak Park. His first painting excursions were to Michigan, Brown County, Indiana, and the Ozark Mountains of Arkansas, where he produced landscapes in oil, watercolor, and intaglio. Constantly in search of new material, Dahlgreen later traveled farther afield, from the Blue Ridge Mountains of North Carolina to Taos, New Mexico and the Yosemite Valley in California. His broadly painted pictures are Impressionist in style with rich, vibrant colors and strong compositions, while his etchings and drypoints are notable for their sinuous lines and bold massing of lights and darks. Both his prints and paintings won numerous awards during his career, bringing him national recognition.

Frank Virgil Dudley (1868–1957)

During his lifetime Frank Virgil Dudley earned the title "Painter of the Dunes" for his single-minded devotion to his favorite subject, the Indiana Dunes along the southern shore of Lake Michigan. The landscapes that he painted of this unique envi-ronment garnered him numerous awards during his lifetime and firmly established his artistic reputation. Dudley was born in Delavan, Wisconsin. He learned the rudiments of art from his father before moving to Chicago, where he attended the city's Art Institute (1886–93). About 1912, during an autumn hike, he discovered the Indiana Dunes and was overwhelmed by their wildness. During the next few years he painted every aspect of the dunes, in the process becoming both a conser-vationist and an outspoken advocate for their preservation. About 1921 Dudley built a small cabin and studio in the dunes near Waverly Beach, where he and his wife would spend nine months of each year. The many paintings that he produced there combine naturalistic description with a subtle poetic quality, suggesting his deep emotional connection with his sub-ject. Depicting every season of the year, these pictures vividly capture the area's ever-changing moods, as well as its solitude and sense of desolation. Thanks in part to Frank Dudley's efforts and to his art, the state assured the preservation of the dunes in 1923 by creating the Indiana Dunes State Park.

Ruth Van Sickle Ford (1897–1980)

A painter in oil and watercolor who created landscapes, still lifes, and portraits, as well as a teacher and administrator, Ruth Van Sickle Ford played an important role in the Chicago art world from the 1930s through the 1960s. She was born in Aurora, Illinois, and studied at the Chicago Academy of Fine Arts, at the summer school of New York's Art Students League, held in Woodstock, New York, and privately. Her teachers included George Bellows, John Carlson, Frederick Swift Case, Bruce Crane, Jonas Lie, Carl N. Werntz, and Guy Wiggins. Ford began her teaching career at age twenty-four, when she became an instructor at the Chicago Academy of Fine Arts, a progressive school that later merged with the School of the Art Institute of Chicago. One of her fellow students was the Chicago native Walt Disney. In 1925 the artist exhibited for the first time at the annual of the Art Institute of Chicago. She would participate regularly in Art Institute annuals in the decades that followed. From 1937 until 1960 Ford was the president and director of the Chicago Academy, while maintaining her role as a teacher. She was one of the founders of the Chicago Women's Salon. In 1961 she became the first woman member of the Chicago Palette and Chisel Club, and she was the first woman member from Illinois of the American Watercolor Society.

Frederic Frary Fursman (1874–1943)

Frederic Frary Fursman was a Chicago-based Impressionist painter who was associated with the artists' colony at Saugatuck, Michigan. Born in El Paso, Illinois, he studied at the School of the Art Institute of Chicago (1897–98, 1901–6), at the Chicago Art Academy (ca. 1896), and at the Académie Julian in Paris (1906–9). While abroad, he spent summers in the French town of Etaples and at various locales in Brittany. After returning to Chicago in 1909, he created vibrant images of the female figure in the outdoors that were similar to those of the American artists working concurrently in Giverny, France, such as Frederick Frieseke and Louis Ritman. In the early twentieth century, Fursman was one of the most popular art instructors in the Midwest. He taught at the Art Institute of Chicago and at the Wisconsin School of Art in Milwaukee. In 1910 he and another Chicago-based artist, Walter Marshall Clute, established the Saugatuck, or Ox-Bow, Summer School. Fursman continued to run the school after Clute's death in 1915. At some point during Fursman's years at its helm, the school became affiliated with the Art Institute of Chicago. Between 1902 and 1939 Fursman was a frequent contributor to annual exhibitions at the Art Institute of Chicago. He received several honors in the course of his career, including prizes from the Art Institute of Chicago in 1911 and 1923 and a medal from the Chicago Society of Artists in 1924.

James Farrington Gookins (1840–1904)

James Farrington Gookins was primarily a landscapist who painted views of the Midwest, the Rocky Mountains, and the Swiss, Austrian, and Italian Alps. He also depicted portraits and flowers, and was one of the few American painters of his generation to paint imaginative fairy subjects. Born in Terre Haute, Indiana, Gookins's artistic career got under way during the Civil War, when he made battle sketches of Indiana soldiers for *Harper's Weekly* and studied briefly with the painter James Henry Beard in Cincinnati (1862–63). In 1865 he moved to Chicago, where, with the exception of trips to the West in 1866 and 1868, he remained until 1870, when he went to Munich for three years of study at the Royal Academy. Returning to Chicago, he taught at the Chicago Academy of Design, where his students included J. Francis Murphy, who became a prominent Tonalist landscape painter. Four years later, Gookins and a fellow painter, John Love, established the Indiana School of Art in Indianapolis, the first professional art school in the state. When the school was forced to close in 1879, he went back to Terre Haute, residing there until 1883, when he made Chicago his permanent home. In the following years, Gookins painted infrequently, devoting much of his time to writing articles and essays and making sketches for newspapers and periodicals such as *Pall Mall*, *Art Review* and *Knickerbocker Magazine*. In 1888 he became a partner at Eldredge & Gookins, a Chicago real estate firm, and thereafter devoted much of his time to civic projects, including helping design a plan for Chicago's downtown subway system.

Frederic Milton Grant (1886–1959)

The painter, illustrator, and etcher Frederic Milton Grant was born in Sibley, Iowa. He initially pursued a degree in architecture, but when he decided to study art, he moved to Chicago and enrolled at the School of the Art Institute and at the Chicago Academy of Fine Arts. He continued his training in Venice, Italy, under William Merritt Chase. Encouraged by the receipt of a prize from Chase, Grant continued his studies in Paris at the Académie Colarossi. On completing his sojourn in Europe, Grant returned to Chicago. Although he was at first inspired by the work of Adolphe Monticelli, he soon turned for inspiration to the vibrant color of Claude Monet's art and the interest in structure and form in the art of Paul Cézanne. Gradually he formulated a decorative Cubist style similar to that of French painters Elie Faure and Amédée Ozenfant. Grant's general approach was to create sketches and watercolor "notes" of landscapes and urban sites that he would convert into large-scale abstract paintings in his studio. In Chicago Grant received local acclaim. The *Chicago Tribune* critic Eleanor Jewett termed him Chicago's greatest colorist, noting that "his work is famous for its magnificent color and fine design. He is probably the greatest of colorists Chicago has ever had." Grant moved to Oakland, California, in the 1950s. He exhibited often at the Art Institute of Chicago and received many awards, including the Popular Prize from the Art Institute (1918).

James Jeffrey Grant (1883–1960)

James Jeffrey Grant was a Chicago sculptor, painter, and engraver who specialized in Impressionist harbor, coastal, and street scenes. He was born in Aberdeen, Scotland, and received his first art training there at Gray's School of Art. In 1904 he moved to Toronto, where he worked as an engraver and sign painter. Three years later he settled in Chicago, where he continued to create engravings and began to exhibit his paintings. He debuted at the Art Institute of Chicago in 1913;

he would show there annually until 1949. He also displayed his work at the Palette and Chisel Club, Chicago, the Pennsylvania Academy of the Fine Arts, Philadelphia, and the National Academy of Design, New York. Grant appears to have traveled extensively, painting in Brittany, on the island of Capri, in his native Scotland, and in Munich, where he studied during 1926–27. He also worked in Gloucester, Massachusetts, painting old fisherman's shacks, schooners, and marine subjects. Grant was a member of the Chicago Art Club, the North Shore Art Association, and the Palette and Chisel Club, Chicago.

Oliver Dennett Grover (1860–1927)

Oliver Dennett Grover was born and raised in Earlville, Illinois, seventy-five miles west of Chicago. He studied law at the University of Chicago and art at the Chicago Academy of Design. Supported by an endowment from his family, at the age of eighteen, he gave up his law studies to go to Europe. He studied in Munich at the Royal Academy (1879), in Florence with Frank Duveneck (1881), and in Paris at the Académie Julian (1882–5). He traveled abroad many times in the course of his career, but after 1885 his base was in Chicago. There he painted portraits and landscapes and produced decorative designs, including murals for the Chicago World's Columbian Exposition (1893), the Branford Memorial Library, Connecticut (1896), and the Blackstone Memorial Library, Chicago (1903). The artist taught at the School of the Art Institute of Chicago (1887–92) and was an organizer and president of the Society of Chicago Artists and of the Society of Western Artists.

John Olson Hammerstad (1842–1925)

John Olson Hammerstad was an expatriate Norwegian artist whose many paintings of mountains, forests, lakes, fjords, and the sea recall the topography of his native land. Originally from Kristiansund, on the Norwegian Sea, he initially trained as a house painter and decorator. In 1863 he won a free tuition grant to study at Johan Frederik Eckersberg's Academy of Painting in Christiania (Oslo), where he remained for three years. He immigrated to the United States in 1869 and settled in Chicago. It was here that he began to paint scenes of Norway drawn from his childhood memories, intended in part, perhaps, to appeal to that city's Scandinavian community. Hammerstad rarely exhibited his work, and little is known about his life. Some of his paintings have a surreal quality to them, sug-gested by the contrast between their tightly painted foreground details and their atmospheric backgrounds. In this respect, they resemble the romantic work by the Norwegian artist Lars Hertervig. Hammerstad eventually turned his attention to the American landscape, producing images with the detailed naturalism favored by Albert Bierstadt and Frederic Church.

Lucie Hartrath (1867–1962)

One of the finest women Impressionists working in Chicago during the early twentieth century, Lucie Hartrath won acclaim for her portrayals of Brown County, Indiana. She was especially admired for her autumnal scenes, which reveal her fine sense of color and compositional design. Born in Boston, Hartrath spent her childhood in Cleveland and attended finishing school in Chicago. She later studied at the School of the Art Institute of Chicago (1894–5, 1898) and in Paris (1898–1900). Hartrath served as head of the Department of Drawing and Painting at Rockford College in Illinois during 1902–04, after which time she went back to Europe, traveling for a year before going to Munich to continue her training under Angelo Jank. Returning to Chicago in 1908, she began making seasonal trips to Indiana, depicting the picturesque scenery in and around Nashville, in Brown County. The recipient of numerous awards and honors at Chicago exhibitions, Hartrath's modified Impressionist style was well received by local art audiences.

Rudolph Frank Ingerle (1879–1950)

Rudolph Frank Ingerle's love of the outdoors and the mountains proved an essential element in his career as a landscape painter. Born in Vienna, Austria, Ingerle had at first expected to become a professional musician. When he was twelve years old he and his family immigrated, eventually settling in Chicago. Ingerle became interested in art and studied at both the John Francis Smith Art Academy and the School of the Art Institute of Chicago. His early canvases often depict views of Brown County, Indiana, and his moonlit landscape scenes became especially popular. In 1914 the artist toured the Ozark Mountains in Missouri, and his enthusiasm for the unspoiled hills, streams, and forests of this region inspired him to produce colorful pictures over the course of a decade. About 1925 he discovered the Great Smoky Mountains of North Carolina and eastern Tennessee. Entranced by their beauty and wildness, Ingerle devoted all his efforts to painting these mountains. Employing a decorative, naturalistic style that eschewed individual detail for more generalized forms, he managed to capture the inherent beauty and grandeur of this scenic range. He became known as the "Master of the Smokies," and his pictures won numerous prizes and awards. Although Ingerle was primarily a landscape painter, he also depicted the local life and people of the mountains in portrayals that are both lively and sincere. His personal efforts proved instrumental in having the United States government set aside the Smokies as a national park.

Wilson Henry Irvine (1869–1936)

Recognized for his poetic renderings of the Connecticut countryside, Wilson Henry Irvine was born on a farm near Byron, Illinois. After graduating from high school in 1888, he moved to Chicago, working as an airbrush artist until 1891, when he became manager of the art department of the Chicago Portrait Company. From 1895 to 1902 he took evening classes in figure painting at the School of the Art Institute of Chicago. During this period, he honed his skills as a landscapist by making sketching trips to rural Illinois and coastal New England. He began exhibiting at the Art Institute annuals in 1900 and soon achieved renown in local art circles. He belonged to many Chicago clubs and societies, and from 1915 to 1918 served as chairman of the Chicago Commission for the Encouragement of Local Art. In 1914 he began summering in Old Lyme, Connecticut, a popular Impressionist artists' colony that became his permanent home in 1918. Irvine painted intimate views of regional scenery throughout the seasons, becoming especially adept at conveying the lush atmospheric conditions of spring. He also painted in Europe, England, and Québec, but Old Lyme and its environs remained his primary painting ground for over two decades.

Alfred Jansson (1863–1931)

Alfred Jansson was an expatriate Swedish artist whose snow scenes of rural Illinois earned him a number of awards and prizes during his lifetime. Jansson was born in Arvika in Värmland, Sweden. He first studied art at the Technological Institute in Stockholm before attending the Christiania Royal Academy in Oslo. After continuing his studies in Paris for two years, Jansson immigrated to the United States in 1889 and settled in Chicago. His reputation grew quickly, and he was awarded a mural commission to decorate the Swedish Building at the World's Columbian Exposition in 1893. Until his death in 1931, Jansson was active in many local art organizations and exhibited his work both in Chicago and throughout the United States. His paintings are based on close observation and executed in a loose, impressionistic style. Full of light and color, these canvases are notable for their spontaneity and freshness. While scenes of thick woodlands blanketed in snow were Jansson's favorite subjects, the artist developed a wide range of landscape views depicting all the seasons of the year.

John C. Johansen (1876–1964)

One of the most celebrated portraitists of his generation, John C. Johansen enjoyed a long and successful career that involved periods of activity in both Chicago and New York. Born in Copenhagen, Denmark, he attended the School of the Art Institute of Chicago from 1891 to 1897. He also studied in Cincinnati with the realist painter Frank Duveneck and then made an extended visit to Paris, attending classes at the Académie Julian and studying briefly with James McNeill Whistler at the Académie Carmen. Returning to Chicago in 1901, he taught at the Art Institute while spending his summers at the Oxbow artists' colony in Saugatuck, Michigan, where he painted landscapes and domestic interiors of women and children. By 1905, the year he married the portrait painter Margaret (Jean) MacLane (1878–1964), Johansen had made a name for himself in Chicago art circles, winning a number of prizes at local exhibitions. In 1908 he moved to New York, where he became a leading portraitist. He was especially adept at male portraiture, drawing his clientele from the fields of religion, business, politics, education, and medicine. A member of the foremost art organizations of his day, he won important awards and prizes throughout his career and continued to paint well into his old age.

Carl R. Krafft (1884–1938)

Carl R. Krafft was one of a group of American landscapists— among them Daniel Garber and Lawrence Mazzanovich— who depicted regional scenery in a decorative Impressionist style at the turn of the twentieth century. Drawing his subject matter from the Midwest, especially the Ozark Mountains of south-central Missouri, Krafft produced lyrical landscapes that brought him acclaim in Chicago and in art centers in the East. A native of Reading, Ohio, he was trained at the School of the Art Institute of Chicago and at the Chicago Academy of Fine Arts. In 1908 he joined the Brown County art colony, near Nashville, Indiana, where he painted landscapes until 1912, when he discovered the colorful scenery of the Ozarks. In the following years he made seasonal visits to that region, establishing an artists' colony that attracted Impressionist painters from Chicago, St. Louis, and elsewhere. Krafft painted in the Ozarks until the mid-1920s. He then worked around Palas Park and Willow Springs, southwest of Chicago. Although landscape remained his forte, he also produced still lifes, marines, portraits, and nudes, exhibiting his work in Chicago as well as in New York, Philadelphia, and Washington, D.C. Krafft retained an allegiance to Chicago, spending his entire career in and around that city.

Walter Krawiec (1889–1982)

Walter Krawiec is perhaps best known today for his work as an illustrator and cartoonist. But he was also an accomplished artist who produced landscapes and portraits and specialized for a time in painting circus scenes. Krawiec was born in Morzewo, Poland but immigrated to the United States with his parents when he was three years old. The family settled in Chicago, where Krawiec attended the St. John Cantius School. Here he developed an interest in drawing that he later pursued by attending classes at the city's Art Institute. He eventually joined the staff of Chicago's *Polish Daily News*. Working his way up, Krawiec became an editorial cartoonist for the newspaper and spent the next fifty years commenting on social, political, and cultural events and affairs, both local and international. His amusing, satirical cartoons were a front-page feature, and in 1962 the newspaper named him Man of the Year and awarded him the Veritas et Caritas (Truth and Charity) Medal. During his career as a cartoonist, he also found time to paint. In a series of circus scenes executed during the 1930s, such as *Fun Maker* (ca. 1935; location unknown), Krawiec focused on the wry but unexpected moments of carnival life.

Lawrence Mazzanovich (1872–1959)

Lawrence Mazzanovich was an exponent of decorative Impressionism, a style that became popular among a number of regionalist painters during the early twentieth century. Following periods of study at the School of the Art Institute of Chicago, the Art Students League of New York, and in Paris,

Mazzanovich settled in Westport, Connecticut, about 1909. He became the town's leading landscapist, depicting local scenery as well as views of northern New England. Although his paintings were essentially representational and light and color were primary aesthetic concerns, Mazzanovich sought to convey a symbolic response to landscape through the use of strong patterning and simplified forms—a deliberate, often non-naturalistic mode of painting that links him with late Impressionism. About 1923 the artist left Westport and moved to Tryon, North Carolina, where he applied his distinctive style to views of the scenery in that locale. Mazzanovich's landscapes were popular among contemporary collectors: as well as exhibiting in the East, he maintained his connections with Chicago through exhibitions at both the Thurber Galleries and O'Brien's Gallery.

Royal Hill Milleson (1849–1935)

Royal Hill Milleson came rather late to art, but his very colorful, light-filled landscapes have earned him a secure place among early twentieth-century American painters. He was born in Batavia, Ohio, but little is known about his life. During the early 1860s he became a journeyman printer but soon gave up that profession to work as a newspaper cartoonist and illustrator for some thirty years. He later turned his attention to art and studied with George W. Morse in Melrose, Massachusetts. About 1900 he settled in Chicago and there attended the John Francis Smith Art Academy. He also became a member of the Chicago Society of Artists and exhibited with that group regularly. In 1912 he wrote *The Artist's Point of View* (Chicago: A. C. McClurg), a series of letters in which he discussed his ideas about art, composition, and color. Some of Milleson's early paintings display certain Tonalist qualities, but his later work is more impressionistic and celebrates nature's rich colors and beauty. His depictions of mountains are particularly impressive.

Minnie Harms Neebe (1873–1936)

A painter, craftswoman, and lecturer, Minnie Harms Neebe studied at the School of the Art Institute of Chicago and with Charles W. Hawthorne in Provincetown, Massachusetts. Among her teachers were E. Ambrose Webster, Walter Ufer, Wellington Reynolds, and Louis Neebe. She exhibited colorful landscapes, floral subjects, and scenes of outdoor leisure activity at the annuals of the Art Institute of Chicago sporadically from 1914 to 1932 and with other local organizations such as the Chicago Society of Artists. Neebe had one-person shows at the Chicago Galleries Association in 1926 and at the Midland Club (Chicago) in 1930. She executed a decorative mural commission for the Karcher Hotel in Waukegan, Illinois, in 1930.

Pauline Palmer (1867–1938)

In addition to painting portraits of leading members of Chicago society, Pauline Palmer produced Impressionist-inspired landscapes, figural subjects, and beach scenes that brought her widespread acclaim. Born Pauline Lennards in McHenry, Illinois, she studied at the School of the Art Institute of Chicago and at the Académies Grande Chaumière and Colarossi in Paris, where her teachers included the American Impressionist figure painter Richard Miller. She also received instruction from Charles Hawthorne during summer trips to Provincetown, Massachusetts. From 1896 to 1938 Palmer exhibited annually at the Art Institute of Chicago, where she received the Marshall Field Prize in 1907, the Thompson Prize (1914), and the Carr Prize (1917). A leading force in the city's thriving art life, she belonged to the Chicago Club, the Chicago Municipal Art League, the Chicago Art Guild, the Chicago Galleries Association, the Chicago Woman's Salon, the Chicago Association of Painters and Sculptors, and the Chicago Art League, where she had the distinction of being the first woman president. After her husband died in 1920, Palmer worked primarily in Cape Cod, painting dunescapes and marines. Known as "Chicago's Painter Lady," the artist passed away while visiting Trondheim, Norway, in the summer of 1938.

Arthur Parton (1842–1914)

Born and raised in Hudson, New York, Arthur Parton studied under the American Pre-Raphaelite painter William Trost Richards in Philadelphia from 1859 to 1861. By the mid-1860s, he had settled in Manhattan, where he became a respected landscapist, exhibiting views of the Adirondack and Catskill mountains at the National Academy of Design, the American Water Color Society, and elsewhere. Parton initially painted in the detailed manner associated with the mid-century Hudson River School, but during the 1880s he adopted a broader, more suggestive technique inspired by the example of the French Barbizon School. His late landscapes consist primarily of views of upstate New York and New England as well as depic-

tions of Scottish scenery. Parton was the recipient of many awards and honors, including a gold medal at the Competitive Prize Fund Exhibition in New York (1878) and the Temple Medal from the Pennsylvania Academy of the Fine Arts (1889). A modest, unassuming artist, he was described by one commentator as an "indefatigable worker" whose "production of landscapes . . . [was] correspondingly great." Parton's brothers, Ernest and Henry, were also successful painters.

Lilla Cabot Perry (1848–1933)

A painter of portraits, figures, and landscapes, Lilla Cabot Perry was an influential figure in the Boston art world at the turn of the last century and one of the few women to combine a successful professional career with the demands of family life. Born in Boston, she married Thomas Sergeant Perry, a writer-scholar, in 1874. In 1887, after studying art in Boston with Alfred Q. Collins, Robert Vonnoh, and Dennis Miller Bunker, she went to Paris, continuing her training at the Académies Julian and Colarossi until 1889. Thereafter, she resided primarily in Boston but spent intermittent summers (1889–1909) in Giverny, the Impressionist artists' colony in France, where she became friendly with Claude Monet and was influenced by his use of high-keyed colors and broken brushwork. One of Boston's most distinguished painters, she exhibited in major exhibitions throughout the United States and Europe. She also helped disseminate Impressionism by promoting the work of Monet and many American practitioners of that aesthetic. Perry was the author of "Reminiscences of Claude Monet from 1889 to 1909" (1927) and four books of poetry. After 1910, she spent her summers in Hancock, New Hampshire.

Frank Charles Peyraud (1858–1948)

Considered one of Chicago's foremost landscapists at the turn of the twentieth century, Frank Charles Peyraud was born in Bulle, Switzerland. Initially trained as an architect, he studied at the Ecole des Beaux-Arts in Paris from 1878 to 1880, after which time he immigrated to the United States. He lived briefly in New York before settling in Chicago in 1881, resuming his formal training at the School of the Art Institute of Chicago. Inspired by both the Barbizon tradition and Impressionism, Peyraud painted intimate rural landscapes—especially scenes of twilight—characterized by broadly defined forms and radiant colors. With the exception of periods of residence in Peoria,

Illinois, New York City, and Wheaton, Illinois, he spent his career in Chicago, exhibiting his work at the annuals of the Art Institute, the Chicago Water Color Club, the Chicago Society of Artists, and elsewhere. He had numerous one-man exhibitions, including shows at the Thurber Art Galleries, the Art Institute of Chicago, O'Brien's Gallery, and the Chicago Galleries Association. In addition to his activity as an easel painter, the artist also produced cycloramic paintings and murals.

Allen Philbrick (1879–1964)

Allen Philbrick was a respected landscape painter, best known for his colorful portrayals of Michigan and Maine. Born in Utica, New York, he studied at the School of the Art Institute of Chicago and at the Académies Julian and Colarossi in Paris. Returning to Chicago in 1906, he joined the faculty of the Art Institute, where he taught composition, drawing, etching, and anatomy for almost five decades. Philbrook spent his summers painting landscapes in Damariscotta, Maine (1908–18, 1932–60) and in White Lake, Michigan (1918–32). He initially worked in a dark, painterly style but later adopted a divisionist technique characterized by bright, pure colors. During the mid-1930s, his work became increasingly realistic. Later in his career, Philbrook worked primarily in watercolor. In addition to his work as a teacher and easel painter, he produced many etchings and painted decorative murals for the Juvenile Court in Chicago, Lake View High School, Chicago, the People's Trust & Savings Bank in Cedar Rapids, Iowa, and the Iowa State Historical Museum.

Tunis Ponsen (1891–1968)

A notable figure in the history of midwestern regionalism, Tunis Ponsen painted a variety of subjects, ranging from portraits, figures, and flowers to rural landscapes, urban scenes, and studio interiors. Described as one of Chicago's "more intelligent and diligent painters," he was affiliated with the conservative faction of that city's thriving art scene. Born in Wageningen, Holland, Ponsen studied art in his homeland before immigrating to the United States in 1913. He eventually settled in Muskegon, Michigan, where he worked as a house painter, decorator, and paperhanger while painting in his spare time and attending evening art classes with Wilbur C.

Kensler at the Hackley Art Gallery (now the Muskegon Museum of Art). In 1924 he moved to Chicago and studied at the School of the Art Institute under Karl Buehr, George Oberteuffer, and Leon Kroll. On winning a scholarship in 1928, he spent a year abroad, after which he returned to Chicago and participated in local and regional exhibitions. As well as depicting the streets and architecture of Chicago, small towns in rural Illinois, and other regional subjects, Ponsen painted landscapes on summer trips to such popular artists' haunts as Provincetown and Cape Ann, Massachusetts, Boothbay Harbor, Maine, and Québec's Gaspé Peninsula. He had one-man shows at the Hackley Art Gallery in 1922, 1923, 1925, 1927, 1931 and 1967. In 1994, a major exhibition—*The Lost Paintings of Tunis Ponsen (1891–1968)*—was organized by the Muskegon Museum of Art and circulated to museums and art galleries throughout Michigan and Illinois.

Louis Ritman (1889–1963)

A talented figure and landscape painter, Louis Ritman was born in Kamenets-Podolski, Russia, in 1859. He studied art in Chicago and Philadelphia before traveling in 1909 to Paris, where he continued his training at the Ecole des Beaux-Arts and familiarized himself with recent French art, especially Impressionism and Post-Impressionism. In 1911 he made this first visit to the Anglo-American art colony in Giverny, where he fraternized with a group of American figure painters that included Frederick Frieseke and Richard Miller. Inspired by their example, he began painting attractive women in domestic interiors or sunlit flower gardens, working in a decorative Impressionist style characterized by lively patterning and highly structured compositions. Ritman spent thirteen summers in Giverny, producing monumental canvases of a very intimate nature. His work was exhibited regularly in Paris and in the United States, attracting the attention of critics such as C. H. Waterman, who in 1919 lauded Ritman's "fine synthesis of colour, beautiful surface and rich composition," and described his canvases as "tender and charming in sentiment, well felt and sensitive in execution." Ritman remained in France until 1930, when he returned to Chicago and began teaching at the School of the Art Institute of Chicago. During the 1950s and until his death in Winona, Minnesota, in 1963, he painted landscapes in southeastern Michigan.

Torey Ross (1875–1966)

A painter and illustrator who specialized in harbor and nocturnal scenes, Torey Ross was born in Gothenburg, Sweden. By 1907 he was living in Chicago. He exhibited that year for the first time at the Art Institute of Chicago; he would participate frequently in Art Institute annuals until 1927. Ross also showed at the Salons of America and the Society of Independent Artists. He was a member of the Chicago Society of Artists. From the mid-1920s through the 1930s, he focused on Chicago's urban and industrial sites, painting in a realist style tempered by a Tonalist aesthetic.

George F. Schultz (1869–1950)

A respected figure in the Chicago art world for over three decades, George F. Schultz painted landscapes and marines, working in a style that conjoined elements of Tonalism and Impressionism. He was born in Chicago, but little is known about his background other than the fact that he studied at the School of the Art Institute of Chicago during 1892. He began submitting oils and watercolors to the Institute's annuals as early as 1889 and did so regularly until 1925, exhibiting landscapes and seascapes painted in and around Chicago, as well as in Maine, Mexico, Illinois, and Indiana. Schultz showed at other local venues, too, including the Palette and Chisel Club and the Arché Club. He had many one-man shows in Chicago, including exhibitions at the Thurber Galleries, the Art Institute of Chicago, Marshall Field & Company Gallery, and O'Brien's Gallery. Along with his partner, the artist William Wilson Cowell, Schultz operated an art and curio shop in Chicago.

Walter Shirlaw (1838–1909)

A prominent figure in the American art world in the late nineteenth century, Walter Shirlaw was a painter of genre scenes, figural imagery, and portraits as well as a muralist and engraver. His early works were realist images, rendered in the dark, painterly mode of the Munich School. Later in his career, he became known for decorative paintings and murals, in which he merged the classicizing approach of the academy with an Impressionist-inspired execution. Shirlaw was born in Paisley, Scotland, and grew up in New York City. From 1865 until 1870 he lived in Chicago, where he worked for the Western Bank Note and Engraving Company of Chicago and played a significant role in the establishment of the Art Institute of Chicago. In 1870 Shirlaw went to Munich to pursue a career as a painter. In the seven years that followed he studied at the Munich Royal Academy and joined American artists including Frank Duveneck who painted in the southern Bavarian town of Polling. On his return to New York, Shirlaw became one of the founders and the first president of the Society of American Artists, taught at the newly founded Art Students League, and supported himself as a magazine illustrator for *Century* and *Harper's Monthly* magazines. By the early 1890s he was active as a muralist, producing works in this genre for private residences and public institutions. In 1890 he was one of five artists sent to take a census among Native Americans. Shirlaw died while visiting Madrid in 1909. Memorial exhibitions of his work were held in New York, Buffalo, Boston, Washington, D.C., Pittsburgh, Chicago, and St. Louis.

John Adams Spelman (1880–1941)

John Adams Spelman is best remembered today for his brilliantly painted landscapes of the American hinterlands. A native of Owatonna, Minnesota, he received private painting lessons when he was ten years old. After studying at the Minneapolis Museum of Art about 1900, he settled in Chicago, where he attended the city's Art Institute. Spelman was a hunter, trapper, and fisherman, and his love of the outdoors and the wilderness drew him to landscape painting. He also produced portraits and even the occasional mythological work. Many of his pictures are impressionistic in style and employ rich color, broad brushwork, and simplified forms. To heighten their visual impact, the artist often employed strong contrasts of light and dark. Although he traveled and painted throughout the eastern United States, he was increasingly captivated by the relative wilderness of northeastern Minnesota. Here, along the north shore of Lake Superior, near the town of Grand Marais, Spelman painted woodland scenes in every season of the year until his death in 1941.

Anna Lee Stacey (1871–1943)

One of a number of talented women painters working in Chicago during the early twentieth century, Anna Lee Stacey was born in Glasgow, Missouri. She received her artistic training at the School of the Art Institute of Chicago (1893–99) and at the Académie Delécluse in Paris (1900). Stacey made her debut at the Art Institute annuals in 1895, exhibiting there regularly until 1939. Based in the Tree Studio Building in Chicago, she painted portraits as well as landscapes, figural subjects, and still lifes, working in a conservative Impressionist style. Her oeuvre includes lyrical views of coastal Connecticut, Cape Ann, Massachusetts, and the Grand Canyon. She also painted European subjects inspired by periodic visits to France, Italy, Belgium, and Spain. In 1939 Stacey moved to San Francisco, Two years later she settled in Pasadena, where she died. The artist was married to the landscape painter John Franklin Stacey.

John Franklin Stacey (1859–1941)

Born in Biddeford, Maine, John Franklin Stacey studied at the Massachusetts Normal Art School in Boston, after which he served as supervisor of drawing for public schools in Pittsfield and North Adams, Massachusetts (1881–83). Following this he went to Paris, studying at the Académie Julian from 1883 to 1886. He lived in Boston until 1888, when he accepted a position at the Kansas City School of Design. Stacey moved to Chicago in 1891, and with his wife, the painter Anna Lee Stacey, established a studio in the Tree Studio Building. The artist exhibited Impressionist landscapes and rural scenes—among them views of Wisconsin, France, and coastal New England—at the annuals of the Art Institute of Chicago from 1894 to 1933, winning a number of medals and prizes. He had several one-man shows in Chicago too, including exhibits at the Art Institute of Chicago (1920), the Chicago Galleries Association (1927), Carson, Pirie, Scott and Company Gallery (1928), and O'Brien's Gallery (1931). Stacey remained a well-known figure on the local art scene until the late 1930s, when he moved to California. He died in Pasadena.

Svend Svendsen (1864–1945)

Svend Svendsen painted rural scenes, marine views, and still lifes, as well as winter landscapes characterized by rich colors and clearly defined forms. Critics detected a Nordic sensibility in his work, as well a "fine poetic feeling" and a concern for "subtle atmospheric effect." Born in Nittedal, Norway, Svendsen immigrated to the United States in 1881, settling in Chicago. He worked for a lithography firm for several years, but when his employer closed the business, he decided to pursue a career as an artist. Although some accounts state that he was entirely self-taught, Svendsen attended classes at the School of the Art Institute of Chicago during 1894 and studied at the Académie Delécluse in Paris in 1896. After many years of struggle and hardship, he rose to prominence in Chicago art circles during the mid-to-late 1890s, attracting patronage from such men as Joseph Jefferson, Edward B. Butler, and Clarence Darrow, among others. His winter subjects, inspired by the example of the Norwegian Impressionist Fritz Thaulow, whom he is said to have met while a boy, were especially admired by local art aficionados.

James Topping (1879–1948)

James Topping is best remembered today for his colorful, naturalistic landscapes and his especially impressive treatment of sky and clouds. Topping began his career as a lithographer but took up painting after immigrating to the United States in 1903. He was born in Cleator Moor near the Cumbrian Mountains in northwestern England in 1879 and received his first artistic training at the Cumberland Technical School of Art when he was fifteen. His teacher there was a portrait and figure painter named John Adamson (1865–1918). After moving to Chicago in 1904, Topping attended classes at the School of the Art Institute of Chicago that same year, again in 1909, and regularly between 1912 and 1914. Over the next three decades he exhibited his work widely and won frequent awards and prizes. He was also active in local artist organizations, being a member of the Palette and Chisel Club (as well as sometime treasurer and director), the Lithographers Club, the Oak Park Art League, and the Chicago Painters and Sculptors Association.

Edna Vognild (1877–1961)

A native of Chicago, Edna Vognild was a painter and lecturer who received her formal training at the School of the Art Institute of Chicago under John Johansen and others. She also studied independently in the East, with the painters Charles Hawthorne and Henry Bayley Snell, and attended classes at the Académies Colarossi and Delécluse in Paris. Vognild participated in the annual exhibitions of the Art Institute of Chicago on five occasions between 1914 and 1922, exhibiting portraits as well as views of Paris, France, and Gloucester, Massachusetts. The recipient of a gold medal at the All-Illinois Society of Fine Arts in 1937, Vognild was married to the painter Enoch M. Vognild (1880–1928).

Carl N. Werntz (1874–1944)

Carl N. Werntz played a lively role in Chicago art life during the early twentieth century. In addition to receiving recognition as a painter of landscapes, genre scenes, and allegorical subjects, he was the founder and director of and a teacher at the Chicago Academy of Fine Arts, a liberal arts institution that offered its students a top-rate faculty and access to a wide-ranging curriculum that emphasized progressive ideas. Born in Sterling, Illinois, Werntz studied at the School of the Art Institute of Chicago under John H. Vanderpoel, Frederick Freer, Lawton Parker, and others. He worked as an illustrator of books and periodicals until 1902, when he established the Chicago Academy of Fine Arts, serving as its director and president, as well as an instructor for almost three decades. During this period, he crisscrossed the globe, studying different forms of art, such as Japanese brush painting and Futurism, which he introduced to his students. He participated in exhibitions in Chicago and throughout the Midwest, as well at a number of eastern venues. His travel sketches, exhibited in London, Dublin, Chicago, and New York, were especially popular among art aficionados. In 1945, a year after his death in Mexico City, a memorial exhibition was held at the Chicago Academy of Fine Arts.

ADDITIONAL WORKS IN THE COLLECTION

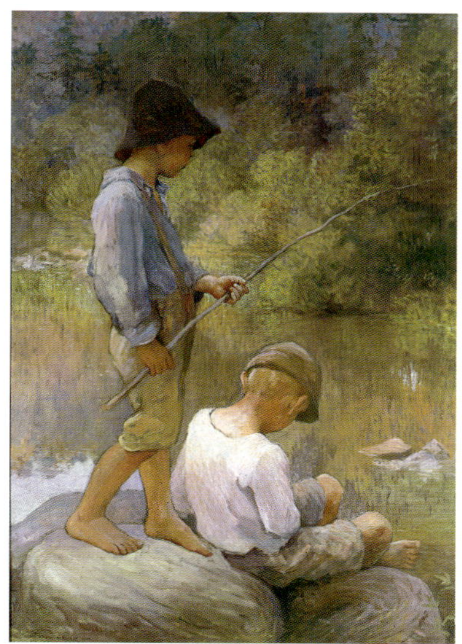

Adam Emory Albright (1862–1957)
Mill Stream, 1912, oil on canvas,
60 × 42 inches

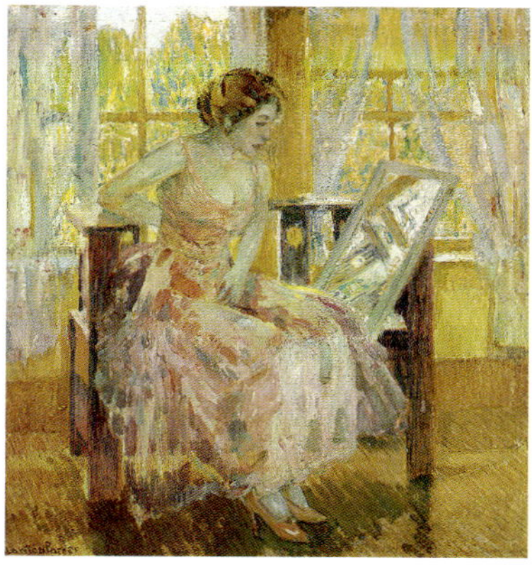

Lawton Silas Parker (1868–1954)
Woman by the Window, ca. 1900,
oil on canvas, 17¾ × 16½ inches

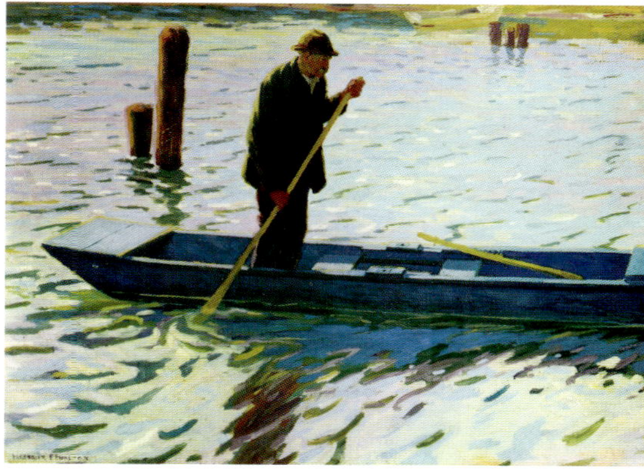

Frederick Frary Fursman (1874–1943) *The Old
Boatsman*, ca. 1910, oil on canvas, 30 × 40 inches

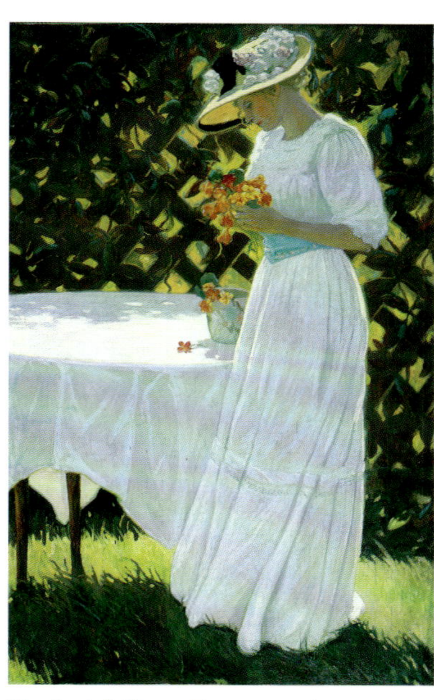

Frederick Frary Fursman (1874–1943)
Nasturtiums, 1911, oil on canvas,
62¼ × 30½ inches

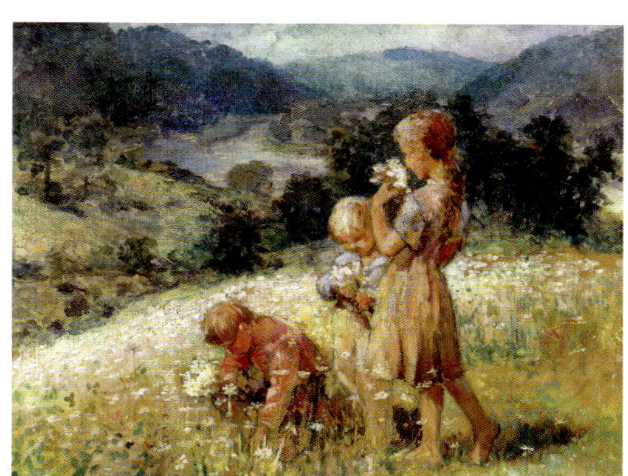

Adam Emory Albright (1862–1957)
Children Picking Daisies, 1911, oil on canvas,
20 × 30 inches

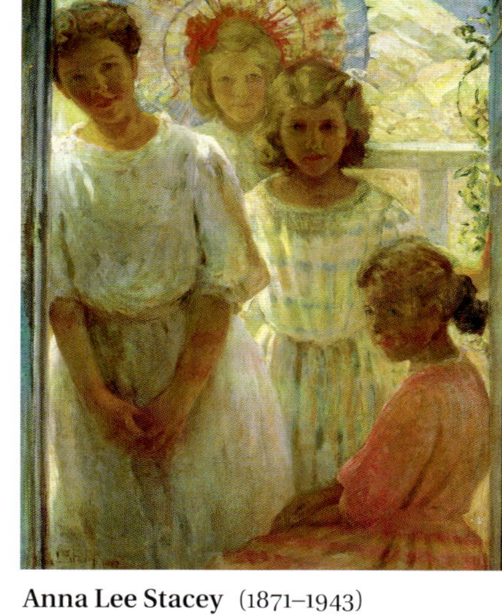

Anna Lee Stacey (1871–1943)
In the Doorway, 1907, oil on canvas,
38 × 29½ inches

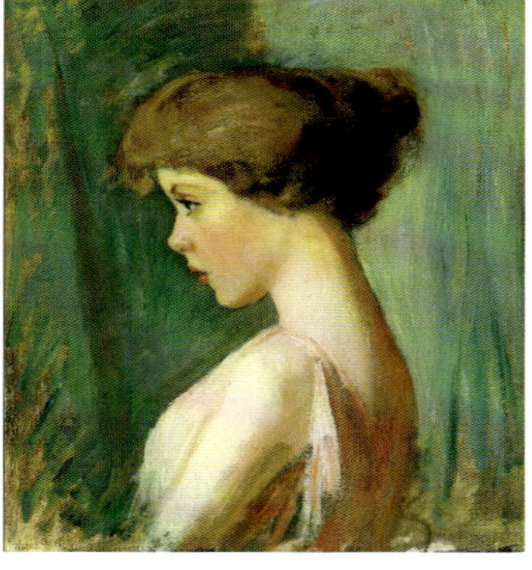

Pauline Palmer (1867–1938)
Young Girl Study, 1910,
oil on canvas, 20 × 18 inches

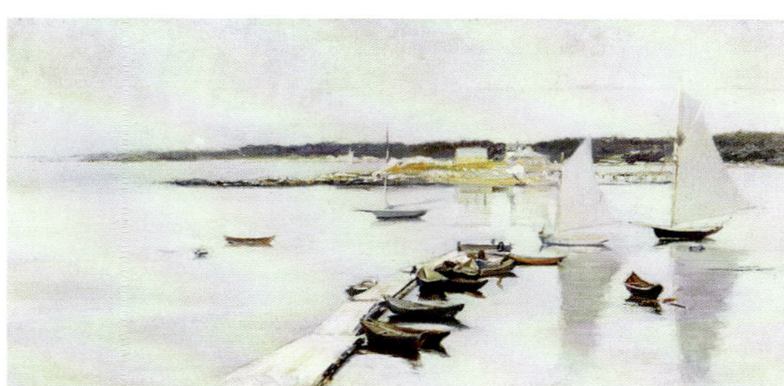

Charles Abel Corwin (1857–1938)
Ten Pound Island, 1900, oil on canvas, 14 × 28 inches

INDEX TO ILLUSTRATIONS